IN THE EYE OF THE GARDEN

Mirabel Osler

IN THE EYE
OF THE GARDEN

J M Dent
London

© Mirabel Osler, 1993

First published 1993

The right of Mirabel Osler to be identified as the author of this work has been asserted by her in accordance with the Copyright, Designs and Patents Act 1988.

Typeset at The Spartan Press Ltd,
Lymington, Hants

Made and printed in Great Britain by Butler & Tanner Ltd,
Frome & London

J M Dent Ltd
The Orion Publishing Group
Orion House
5 Upper St Martin's Lane
London WC2H 9EA

British Library Cataloguing-in-Publication Data

ISBN: 0 460 86141 7

CONTENTS

PREFACE

Don't be misled. I have written about gardens, gardening, flowers, shrubs and trees as a painter uses size to prepare his canvas. The garden works for me as 'a ground plot for the mind' in much the same way as Patrick Leigh Fermor's description of a journey at the age of eighteen was the artery from which flowed ideas way beyond the boundaries of mere mileage. I can't apologize. I enjoy straying. But you may not, so this is to forewarn you. Digressions abound, from giraffes to Odysseus, suffused with a strong scent of violas wafting through the pages.

CHAPTER I

THE ALCHEMY OF GARDENS
Why?

THERE IS AN ELEMENT OF GARDENING WHICH IS never written about in spite of the hundreds of words on the subject that line the shelves of our bookshops. Perhaps this aspect is too insubstantial. Or subjective? Or threatening? And all some gardeners look for is hard advice: for Latin names, flowering months, photographs and vivid descriptions of flowers. Possibly, pursued by expediency and the need for instant effects, harassed by the pressure of living and an overkill of floral advice, gardeners shut out those other voices. For, after all, tunnel vision does keep the mind securely in focus. And for some, eradicating moss from a lawn can, I suppose, be an all-absorbing imperative.

I want to write about the dynamic which, unsuspectedly, I found lying on the other side of planting a tulip. A kind of undertow to gardening which cannot be ignored and which compels me to try to put down in words what has mystified me ever since I first picked up a spade: it's the part of gardening which doesn't show; like the statue in the rock waiting to be hewn by the carver, it lies there quiescent, a passive force which maybe remains undiscovered for years. But for those who are susceptible to this enigma it's as inherent to a garden as a clump of pinks.

Disciplined meditation is the acknowledged route for discovering one's true nature – should you want to.

Gardening does this for me willy-nilly. No sooner am I out there, concerned with whatever trivial or charismatic effect I'm set on, than my mind becomes filled with thoughts that I was not seeking. When I'm on my knees grubbing at the root of things or when I'm digging holes in which to plant a shrub, unasked and from an unperceived direction inconsequential thoughts come into my head. I can be unravelling a clematis, spreading muck, or doing no matter what, when capricious ideas, irrelevant and provoking, drift into my mind in a way that never happens when I am travelling, swimming or ironing. What mysterious percipience lurks about gardens? Why am I ambushed by latent conjectures I never pursued? Submerged, these inklings lie layer upon layer, surfacing from some deep stillness to take me unaware. They rise of their own volition from an unwonted source whose root I have never sought. Why and from where these reflections come is not of my doing; they have nothing to do with me; I was not asking questions.

This is the omnipotence of gardening.

On the practical side it is maddening, especially in winter when my gloves are thick with mud, cold and stiff and impossible to remove. But inveigled, I need to write down these feral thoughts or else, by the time I am back in the house, like dreams they have vanished, leaving only a trace of an idea that provocatively stays out of reach. Now paper and pencil are in my pocket along with the rose ties and nails.

What other creative undertaking can produce such total submission as gardens do? They are both felicitous and predatory; they get you by the throat and do not let go. Surrender is total, so that in the end waiting eleven-and-a-half months for the annual flowering of a transitory rose becomes credible. Fugitive contentment may last only a few days, but while the papery frailty of a group of romneya fills a corner of the garden before a frost annihilates the flowers, there is nothing for it but to stand dumbfounded.

For many of us, scanning a catalogue and knowing little, names are often the first thing to catch the imagination, long before logic. Instinctively, when a rose called 'Cuisse de Nymphe' appears on an order form no one would seriously opt for a thing called 'Peek-a-boo'. Or take 'heartsease'; with a name like that the flower has a head start – quite apart from whether you are after wild pansies or not.

Years ago I planted 'loosestrife' – just for its name – and have been distraught ever since. Its greedy annexation of my pasque flowers, so exquisite and frail with their furry leaves, stems and drooping heads, are no match for the loosestrife's tenacity of life. How ever often I dig up its irascible roots and transplant the piercing yellow flowers to wilder territory, I never stop reproaching my susceptibility to its persuasive name. So now I am more wary, though I may dither about whether to plant 'rue' in the garden with its dire sense of foreboding (in fact the metallic, finely etched foliage is a garden bonus); 'heartsease' does live up to its promise: its endearing disposition really does bring solace to the mood of any faltering gardener.

Gardening is unique in many ways. Not only for the personal aura which it manifests, but because it is an occupation to which there is no end. Gardeners are always on their way, but never arriving. Unlike the poet or the architect, we cannot walk away from our creations. What a writer writes remains on the page, the painter's brushwork, the architect's building, or the composer's score, passes from one century to another. A garden is temporal.

Yet this is the magic of gardening; we become enthralled however unaware we are of what is stealthily happening while we are dividing irises. Gardening is unique, too, for giving us a second chance. That doesn't often happen in life. You cannot have another go with a job you have bungled, with crucial advice you failed to take, or with high-rise flats you have built; or even with a child you despair of, a husband, or the bailiffs. But gardens, however disastrous, are beneficent. The return of the seasons allows us to try again. Again and again – there is no end.

What failed last summer can be attempted in the next. Even as the flower dies it is preparing for revival in spring. The continual cycle of decay and regeneration gives us forever the opportunity to broadcast fresh seeds, for there is one intrinsic truth: a garden never repeats itself. Never again can you have this year what you achieved in the last.

Gardens and writing about them are new to me. All my life I have written letters because I wanted to. Correspondence with friends has been a kind of self-indulgent form of expression which, during the years we lived in Thailand and Greece, provoked a particularly fruitful incentive to write letters which weren't a chore but a private gratification.

Now that I am writing for publishers my life has become transformed. I have had to alter my stride so much that surprise is an understatement. It is one thing to write a letter to a person one knows, but to write for strangers seemed at first an alien occupation, leaving me adrift and somewhat unfocused. And however flexible publishers appear at the beginning, vowing to let me go my own way, they are always edging me to conformity, demanding little dollops of 'how to' about gardening; suggesting I give advice about siting, acidity or growth rates; nudging me into keeping my sights on climatic zones, on the American, the Australian and the Japanese market. But how can I? I'm not a garden expert in any sense of the meaning, only someone who blunders about in the shrubbery.

M. F. K. Fisher, an American writer, wrote prolifically and most vigorously about eating. Food, wine, kitchens, restaurants, markets, taste, herbs, aromatic spices and nuances of taste rolled through her prose – but Miss Fisher gave few recipies. That was not what one read her for: it was for her descriptions of everything to do with the delightful art of eating. If you wanted a recipe you usually looked elsewhere.

So it is with gardening: I cannot give recipes. Advice on propagation and pruning, nuggets of wisdom or know-how are not in this book, nor will you find sagacity or counsel scattered like slow-release pellets through these pages; I can only write cursorily about what has worked or failed for me in a really very limited experience of gardening. But what I do want to write about lies on the other side of expertise. It has to do with intimacy and atmosphere, with the garden's seasonal fickleness and unsuspected magnetism that is slowly disclosed once you start gardening; qualities which provoke those who make them to speak of their gardens with ardent fervour or an almost sacrosanct devotion. As a gardener quietly remarked, without any rancour, as we walked through her garden in spring: 'No one sees that there are extraordinary plants here. Only I know.'

The way I was taken over was entirely arbitrary. In 1980 my husband Michael and I started to make our first garden out of one-and-a-half acres of rough undulating land with a stream flowing through a pastoral landscape. Later, from exchanging letters with a friend, a writer who gardens in Pennsylvania and who lives and works in New York, I was led into writing articles, reviewing books and finally to writing my own about the making of our country garden; in my late fifties, due entirely to the thrust and encouragement of this American friend and through no incentive of my own, I found I'd meandered into a world I had never thought of entering.

Being receptive to whatever gets at you even when you are looking the other way (more often when you *are* looking the other way), is imperative. Mentally my bag is packed – it has been for years. It lies under my bed in case I hear a footfall, see a shadow fall across the threshold, or reach towards an outstretched hand and a beckoning finger.

So often it is not when you are on the alert, pushing at boundaries, chasing opportunities and anxiously flailing for responses, but when you are unaware or enclosed that the best happens. Lying fallow, or preoccupied with minutiae – no matter which – if a window opens and the prospect pleases, float through it; that window may never open again. And it has nothing to do with age. There are people who are ossified by their mid thirties and others, in their seventies, who still respond to the song of the Lorelei.

Gardening has turned my world upside down. From being a skimmer of gardens, a person who repudiated horticultural demands – damped down for years by animals first and then by children – I found myself thrust involuntarily into the clutch of cultivation. And remaining receptive can apply no more obviously than in this terrain, for to garden you have to keep an open mind.

Most things are never meant, and nowhere is this more apparent than

in a garden. Mental atrophy cannot set in, nor can complacency or self-congratulation, for just when you think everything is shipshape and you are in control, a spontaneous seeding of columbines confounds you with the aerial performance of their blue and lemony petals in flight. Or, quite by chance, self-seeded oriental poppies aggressively stride through a bed of mauve and pink flowers, inadvertently saving the underpowered pastels from being commonplace – the dramatic scarlet changing the mood into one of celebration. And drama in gardens, of one sort or another, is taken for granted. Tragedies happen. Honey fungus and moles. Or gales which fell seventy-year-old trees. Such tragedies test you relentlessly. And sometimes, just when you feel 'that's it', this time I cannot produce enough sanguine detachment to get over this latest blow, your garden smiles benignly and shows how the loss of trees spreads it to the horizons.

The spirituality of gardens has spanned the world. In time and in geography. The mystical quality that a garden throws off is as powerful as the scent of flowers. And evident in every continent. Our responses to the many forces of a garden are as varied and personal as the plants which grow in them. What sings for one person, falls on deaf ears to another. What gives one of us gooseflesh may pass unobserved by the next. Some are transfixed by the austere minimalism of oriental gardens with their unity and feeling of 'oneness'; in contemplating rocks and raked sand or a pavilion and bamboos reflected in a pool, the visitor may find idyllic harmony from introspection and a sense of tranquillity. Others may find unanimity in the geometric water channels of Mughal gardens where formal enclosures, made generations ago, still give a sense of serenity among a landscape of barren rock. The poise of a bough, the shadow of leaves, the dimpling of water can be the apotheosis of these gardens.

Elsewhere in the world the black shade of cypress, the silver of olives, the patina of statues, and a sweet sense of decay, may quicken the heartbeat of others; or responses may quiver to the colonial grandeur of Southern gardens in the United States, to evergreen magnolias and the flush of azaleas. And for a few, the very paucity of flowers among blocks of solid topiary or the melancholic neutrality of winter is when a garden is at its most resonant.

If it is true that gardeners dig no deeper for hidden meaning in their gardens than the need to prepare the ground for a plant, it may be that they do not want to look deeper. The sensuality of a garden is enough. Why ask for more? I do not. Yet, without my consent, the reverse happens. The garden turns on me. Somewhere, invisibly and very powerfully, I am being got at by something very pushy. Whether it is a metaphysical force or merely dotty aberration, I know that when I walk into my garden and start working, I am drawn across an invisible threshold I never knew existed until I began to grovel.

CHAPTER II

WHOSE TREES ARE THESE?
Planting

PLANTING IS A FORM OF HOCUS-POCUS WHICH TURNS out to be real. It satisfies a deep primeval urge to put into the earth something that one day will be manifestly different to what I am holding in my hand: a seed, a slip or an acorn. Whether the seeds are scattered on barren or cultivated land, their potential invades the imagination. The mind's eye is vivid, it can visualize colour radiating through grassland, or more prosaically look forward to pulling up a dishful of radishes.

In *The Man Who Planted Trees* by the French writer Jean Giono, a shepherd carried a bag of acorns and an iron rod so that as he took his sheep to pasture he could thrust the rod into the ground and plant an acorn. Whose land it belonged to was of no consequence; usually it was on communal grazing 'in that ancient region where the Alps thrust down into Provence.' By the end of three years the shepherd had planted one hundred thousand oak trees, of which perhaps ten thousand would burgeon where nothing had grown before. As it is unlikely that any of us will spend our days herding flocks through the valleys and hills of Britain, the Appalachians or the plains of the Murrumbidgee, we cannot make such a grandiose gesture but we could plant one sapling: a catalpa, a myrtle, a swamp cypress or a crab apple with its frothy blossom and fruit glossy as nail varnish.

Trees are the lungs of the garden. Without them a garden gasps for breath. To walk into an established garden where there is not one serious tree is a bitter deprivation: every gardener should feel beholden to plant at least one, however small the space, as a bequest to following generations.

John Evelyn, the seventeenth-century virtuoso, writer, garden designer and, most crucially, guardian angel of trees, came under the spell of French gardens on his protracted travels in Europe. He translated French gardening works, brought the word 'avenue' into our language, as well as having a critical and far-reaching effect on the silviculture of this country. A contemporary of Evelyn's, Stephen Switzer, another writer and garden designer, who was much involved in the layout of Wray Wood at Castle Howard in Yorkshire, graphically described John Evelyn as he who 'first taught Gardening to speak proper English.'

But it was not acorns that had Michael and me springing onto the land on a sunny morning, it was planting trees. Trees were the beginning of our becoming appropriated by the garden. At first we'd only tentatively thought of gardening: we had land, we had a stream, we had alders meandering along it, so it was only natural to want to enhance the uneven land with a few trees and some shrub roses. We did not intend to make a garden, only to do a bit of gardening. Looking back I cannot point to the exact day when we discovered that we had, unintentionally, made a garden. Without ambition or a speck of know-how, we had succumbed to the basic urge which makes anyone with land involuntarily think of planting.

Years later we would walk round our garden, bewildered, wondering how we had been bamboozled. On summer evenings, when the roses were languishing under their heavy-headed blooms and the place was redolent of scents, we would ask: What *have* we done? Whose fault had it been; and into what strange places had our gardening led us? For quite by chance, from taking photographs for our own records, Michael had

been drawn into photography, his productions ending up in prestigious magazines on both sides of the Atlantic. In the strange way that things come at you when you aren't looking for them, seeing gardens through the limitations of the camera's eye began to fascinate Michael. For hours, peering through the lens of a camera, his tripod spread-legged on some hummocky bank in the early morning or at twilight, he'd try to catch a colour, a look, an essence or spirit of something he perceived as precious. One June twelve pages of his photographs appeared in the magazine *The World of Interiors*, as evocative and sensitive as any taken by far more experienced photographers. There was one of our pond, out-of-focus and covering two pages, which gave a blurred appearance of the light in summer as palpable as an Impressionist painting.

But then a garden does have some sort of volatile charge which sends people off at a tangent into other worlds. I know of one gardener who finds perversely that every time he starts to garden he instantly feels an urge to compose. Once indoors he is compelled to sit at the piano and all his plans to prune the philadelphus go up the spout.

The strategy of planting a tree or a shrub rose is profoundly satisfying. It is one of my favourite garden jobs, but it is easier with two than alone. Now that I am making a garden on my own, the prospect doesn't excite me in quite the same way as it used to when Michael and I set out together to plant a tree. From numerous thwarted attempts we learnt how vital it was to have our wits about us. Forethought. That was the essential: the practicality of mentally going through the list of everything we were going to need before we trudged up into the orchard or towards the stream to plant a tree, to say nothing of the dilemma over choosing the right site.

Trees, or the kinds we put in, were going to grow tall. An unconsidered decision to thrust a sapling in a convenient space was not on. Unless we were realistic and thought of the height, branch span and density of foliage that one day this slender little stem of six or seven feet was going to produce, in a few years we would be faced by the whole cumbersome business of transplanting the tree to a more suitable setting. It can be done, and we have done it. Often. In our early days walnuts, maples and tulip trees (whose leaves in autumn seemed to be out of sync, turning colour randomly, some leaves being yellow and brown while the rest were still green) went in here and there with reckless sangfroid, only to be dug up later and transplanted to a better place.

Before we started we needed two wheelbarrows. One was for the earth we excavated, one for the stones we inevitably dug up; a stake, if it were necessary, with a suitable tie to prevent chaffing; compost, leaf mould, friable earth or whatever nourishment we were going to lavish on the tree or rose; a sharp knife to trim any roots that looked sickly or deviant; a fork, a spade, and the plant itself which had been soaking in a bucket of water. What have I forgotten? Gloves, of course, if the rose is a thorny one like 'Albertine' (a prodigious climber with flowers the colour of peachy underwear). Unless you have hands toughened by years of spiny abuse, gloves are the only way to handle this colossus.

Then we began. The bit I liked was after we had dug the hole and measured its depth against the soil mark on the tree. While Michael held the stake and tree upright, I had the solicitous job of unravelling the roots, snaking in every direction, to ensure stability. It seemed such a sanguine task spreading those life-giving threads on compost matured months ago for just this moment; covering the roots with soil while Michael jiggled the tree gently to settle them comfortably in place and firming them in as we shovelled back the barrow-load of earth. Stamping down the loose soil to the original level, tying the tree to the stake, and watering the ground were the last operations before finally standing back and trying to imagine that this unremarkable stick would one day turn into a whitebeam whose half-opened leaves in spring look like the flowers of some glamorous magnolia.

Having read that it wasn't meteorites colliding into our planet that brought organic matter to earth, but that a 'primeval soup may have come from a gentle organic rain of cometary dust . . .', I found that idea delightfully bizarre when planting a tree. Nor would I dream of disputing the proposition that about four billion years ago there could have been no living thing on earth. If it's true that organic rain, originating from asteroids and comets, made a soft landing with the organic molecules intact, then tree-planting becomes a reverential act laced with profound humility.

A good deal of writing consists of finding an alternative word; so it is with gardening. Finding an alternative to replace our first impetuous planting took up a lot of time when it became obvious a career move was imperative for a tree or shrub. Plants fill space in all sorts of ways. I was certainly slow to discover the invaluable effect of verticals – and I don't just mean trees, those are impresarios in a garden – but I mean spires of verbascums, hollyhocks, delphiniums and many others.

If I half-closed my eyes as I looked at the garden, I saw immediately where verticals were paramount. No matter how beautiful the planting was, unless there were vertical lines the design was a flop, whether these lines – shoulder-high uprights or architectural steeples – came from willowy flowers or from tapering evergreens. Unfortunately nothing grows in northern climes in the same way as the inky-dark Italian cypress of the Mediterranean, *Cupressus sempervirens*, whose fastigiate columns add distinguished black strokes to the background of medieval paintings or to the landscape of Greece. The best we can do is to try the false cypress, *Chamaecyparis lawsoniana* 'Kilmacurragh', which looks so majestic in the rose garden at Castle Howard.

Scent and colour in the garden are always being commended, but what of shape? What of outlines, contours, frameworks and tracery? To begin with I never took such forms into consideration and it was only much later that I began to realize how versatile and imperative these features are to a garden. The curves and angles, the solid humps and ethereal billows; the horizontal spreaders making splendid foundations for fussy-leafed volumes of ceanothus and the muslin-lightness of gypsophilas; the hummocky silhouettes of rugosas, bulky as igloos, forming esssential flowerbed mounds; but until there are incisive uprights the garden is as tasteless as a salad without garlic. And why should vertical plants always be herded at the back of the bed where their majestic deportment becomes confused, rather than standing alone in the foreground as decisive pointers beneath which runs away all the more lowly planting? There may be a practical reason: that single plants, unsupported by their peers, fall over on the first gusty day, but with a little contriving two together, standing as a courtly pair, could have an invisible prop at their centre.

A few taller penstemons near the front of a deep bed of flowers immediately lifts the whole look of the planting; their range of colours is so subtle they can be used like watercolours running down a page. Pink or white foxtail lilies make bold brushstrokes in the foreground of whatever lies beyond, and a few ligularias with their openwork spires allow other plants to be seen through their yellow flowers; most of the showy campanulas work well, with their varied blues picking up a scrap of the same colour in something further along the bed. But among the best vertical plants are the verbascums or mulleins, which grow so tall they must be located where their lofty presence makes an emphatic plumb-line. The ungainly great mullein or Aaron's Rod, *Verbascum thapsus*, are so rangy they look magnificent when sparingly planted against a dark background.

The verbascums have a whole clutch of descriptive names including Clown's Lungwort, Cuddy Lugs, Our Lady's Flannel and most imaginatively, Wild Ice Leaf. They are a godsend: either used as decorative sceptres where their dusty or bleached tones, almost the colour of biscuits, look wonderful soaring through flaccid roses, or standing like shafts, their chrome or sulphurous yellow bright above prostrate grey travellers. Most successful for us was the Cotswold hybrid verbascum 'Pink Domino' which lightened the velvety and deep-garnet flowers of the moss rose 'William Lobb'.

Among the other vertical flowers forming modest spikes are such things as the perennial lobelias. From North America there's the somewhat tender *Lobelia cardinalis* with scarlet racemes, and the unsociably named *L. siphilitica* whose late summer cerulean flowers look so good among their bluey-green leaves. The rash inclusion of sunflowers towering over a bed of low clumpy shrubs sprinkled like pincushions under these stately plants can look stunning. Foxgloves with their peripatetic tendencies are a boon; as far as I'm concerned they can seed themselves anywhere. There is a street near me where they have escaped the front garden and grow out of the pavement joints alongside an iron fence. The rigidity of the iron, each post crowned with a spear, makes a perfect foil for the perambulating nature of the pink and cream foxgloves rising from their rosettes of leaves. On an island just off the west coast of France, where I had gone to visit a very eccentric garden for my book on French hidden gardens, the quayside cottages had wild hollyhocks growing to their eaves. As the cottages were colour-washed in pale yellows, blues or pinks the effect of these vagrant flowers looked too pretty for anything.

As for the Himalayan lily, *Cardiocrinum giganteum*, it defies logic in the language of gardens. A Brobdingnagian among bulbs; originating in the desolate wilderness of Tibet, this whopper with dangling white trumpets needs careful siting away from other flowers, not only because of its height (I saw them fifteen feet tall at Inverewe in Scotland) but for its sickly-sweet scent. Take one indoors and you'd back out of the room in a hurry to escape from its overpowering sense of claustrophobia and gloomy reminder of funeral parlours.

For formality, and for the patient gardener, Japanese privet or bay trees grown on stems with their heads browbeaten by regular cropping into spheres make decisive verticals. Their stiff deportment above herbs contrasts effectively with the felty leaves and modulations of green. Standard roses, which are used much more adventurously in France than in Britain, are plants which are not tried out as freely as they deserve. They don't have to stand in a bed of slightly-mounded bare earth looking pitifully marooned encircled by blobby annuals, but can be herded together like a flock of scented ladies wearing preposterous cerise, apricot or ivory hats. And choosing what colours to plant at their feet could soak up hours of winter day-dreaming while rain was overflowing the gutters and the TV was off.

I once read of a tropical plant with spires which were imitated by insects arranging themselves as protective camouflage so perfectly that their varied colours flowed from dark to light in exact semblance of the flower in bloom. The insects still do this – though now on other shrubs; the original plants have been extinct for centuries.

There is a whole gamut of planting mania – whether it is bedding plants for instant propulsion or the long-term contemplative serenity from planting trees. Whichever you choose to do, at the time of planting, you can surrender to that untroubled equilibrium which is at the nub of gardening. The sense of nowness is intensely centripetal. And as long as you are unhurried, the day is still, and you have all the tools and ingredients you need, planting is one of the most therapeutic rituals which will resuscitate the mood of even the most spiritually water-logged.

In northern Thailand, we never did our own gardening; but when we felt in need of vicarious husbandry, we used to go out into the countryside at different times of the year to watch the ritual cycle of rice growing: ploughing, planting, harvesting and threshing.

Soon after the rains began we'd see farmers ploughing their small plots between the irrigation canals, using primitive ploughs with mould-boards of wood often untipped by steel and with long, gracefully curved wooden handles. Very slowly they moved to and fro, each man guiding his water buffalo by a cord through its left nostril; looking across the shallow flooded patches we would watch the upside-down reflection of their unwieldy movement, deliberate and ponderous. Some time in early August rows of men and women transplanted the young seedlings from the rice bed into the field. Continually stooping, while moving in a wavering line, they pushed a few seedlings in at each step.

Later in the year, about November I think, we'd pass the reapers at work. Doubled over as they cut with curved sickles, they would make a curious lifting sweep with their bunches of gathered rice. The effect from a distance was of a rhythmic arm movement as they bent, cut and lifted the sheaves high over their heads to ensure there would be no loss from careless handling. About this time too, we'd often pass groups of men carrying sheaves of rice hung over their carrying poles on their way to the threshing ground. They walked with small steps using a kind of lilting movement, their legs always slightly bent as though the sheaves were unbearably heavy.

As for the threshing, which takes place in December and early

January, we saw it done in two ways: by hand, the sheaves beaten against the ground of the threshing floor, or by animals. In the south we had watched the beautiful sight of two buffaloes walking round and round through the deep rice straw cumbrously treading out the grain like a pair of black somnambulists.

The last part of the rice ritual came when the women, with light and supple movements, winnowed the grain by tossing it up from shallow bamboo trays, the grain falling into one pile and the chaff gently floating into another. Occasionally we'd seen groups of men winnowing; then they used large wooden paddles with which to cast the grain into the air with a ritualistic movement originating in an ancient winnowing dance. Days later we'd overtake high-wheeled carts drawn by oxen carrying the harvested rice to the substantial wooden granaries. Because the harvest was so precious, these storehouses, with deep protective roofs, stood on tall legs often higher than the house. The fascination and the hypnotic contentment from watching the ritual of rice production brought the onlooker a stupefying paralysis because at every phase each task lacked any sense of urgency.

Tending things indoors, compared to tending things out-of-doors, is as different as a cultivated antirrhinum is to a wild one. In a potting shed, with its smell of loam and lime laced with damp mould and a faint thread of acrid rust coiling about the tarry smell of twine, there is a dependable security and calm. The light is filtered, colours are made up of terracotta and every variation of brown in the spectrum; rusting tools lie among dog-eared catalogues – pathetic mementos of abandoned plans; a tress of raffia, ousted by polyvinyl ties, hangs on a nail; mouldering seed packets and mildewed garments grown mossy with age add to the muffled sense of earthy enclosure. From the rafter hangs an ancient trug, its bottom worn threadbare from years of use, and long since replaced by a plastic, lightweight, waterproof and virulent green supermarket affair.

How sad. Potting sheds are an endangered species. Only in old gardens will you still find the genuine article built within the walls of a neglected kitchen garden, where families of lilliputian clay pots for seedlings still lie where they were abandoned decades ago, alongside the cast-iron bobbins once used for lining-up the planting rows in a kitchen garden. Potting sheds should have preservation orders on them: hundreds of years hence archaeologists will find foundations and wonder what sort of person inhabited this miniature house.

Potting, pricking and transplanting outside is altogether different. Your ears are not muffled by silence, but as twitchy as the ears of a submerged hippo. Turtle doves coo, the stream gurgles, bees murmur and if your neighbour's chainsaw or grass 'strimmer' (an environmental pollutant which ought to be banned) is not raising the decibels, the

voice of the cuckoo can be heard calling and responding across the pastoral meadows with the same poignancy of spring as it did in the days of Thomas Hardy.

An altogether different kind of planting takes place in autumn: bulb planting. And unless you are making holes for them in a flower bed, where you handle the silvery and gold bulbs as delicately as marbles on a solitaire board as you place them between other plants, the task can be hell. Backbreaking and arduous; putting hundreds of daffodils or species tulips in grass requires commitment, a kind of mad devotion to the celebration to come. It is only afterwards, when the basket is empty, when you tread back the turf, straighten your back and feel your muscles relax, that you realize that this sort of work, although so different from tree planting, is another of a garden's great hosannas.

'I have to see how they die' is one of the most original ways of choosing what to plant in a garden. It was said to me by a knowledgeable gardener whose place I had visited in midsummer when everything was throbbing with vitality. But dying? Yes, some flowers become more impressive as the season wanes, and to choose hydrangeas and helichrysum, alliums and lavender because they look as good dead as alive turns the choice of flowers on its head. *Iris foetidissima*, for one, is a thing of beauty with its peeling-back pods full of scarlet seeds; astilbes and willow gentians die with delicacy; the modest knotweed has flowers and leaves which turn to the warm colour of rust. And there are roses whose summer brightness fades to sulky tones, or others whose flamboyant hips and leaves, the colour of daffodils, become more radiant as the season seeps away.

So to start a garden with an eye on death becomes a rum approach to filling in a plant catalogue. On that basis, in the end you must be led back to trees. They have been dying for centuries; they are the professionals, not only for their autumn colours, but because when every vestige of leaf has fallen you are left with unadorned basics.

Unadorned basics. It's a thought. Why, if you go to a horticultural society meeting, are most of the members grey-haired women? That sentence looks depressing but deserves jubilation. Those same women, after years of bringing up families, coping with jobs and giving out support from an assumed bottomless well, now at last have time to make a garden. Perhaps for the first time they are living for themselves not for other people; living according to their own values rather than those of others. Freed to take up picture-framing, vernacular architecture, Open University, glass-blowing, Sanskrit or the history of Genghis Khan, whatever it is, by choosing to garden they give themselves spiritual elbow-room.

As a place for self-expression the garden can become an extroverted display, flaunting and triumphant, or a floral retreat of intense intimacy. Here is a personal domain, perceived with unqualified directness, without using someone else's interpretation of what a garden is about. Just outside their own backdoors these gardeners have a world within their grasp.

A French lady who runs a commercial garden crammed to bursting with Old Roses which she and her ebullient husband grow with an insatiable passion, told me that when everyone is gone, including her husband, then is the time she finds the garden speaks to her. In the early morning, or at twilight sitting on a bench among multitudes of roses, she feels she is sovereign of her dominion.

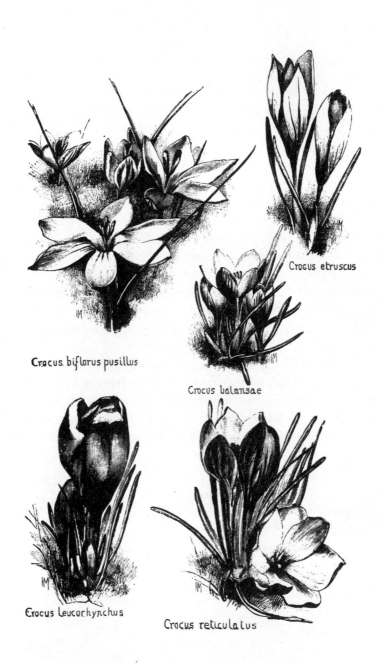

Crocus etruscus

Crocus biflorus pusillus

Crocus balansae

Crocus Leucorhynchus

Crocus reticulatus

CHAPTER III

THE CORRUPTIVE EARTH
FROM WHICH THEY SPRING
Spring

ET'S HAVE A SOCIETY FOR PEOPLE SUSCEPTIBLE TO gooseflesh. How is it that however often you read them certain poems bring you out involuntarily in gooseflesh even though you know beforehand this is liable to happen? Applicants for my society, whether they were poetry, art or music enthusiasts (and for all I know there are foodies whose flesh crinkles at the mere thought of hollandaise sauce), would have to pass a test before being accepted; they would have to prove themselves before the committee by visually demonstrating their puckering flesh. It's not something you can prepare for as in other entrance tests: you cannot deliberately bring a blush to your cheek, force hiccups, a sneeze or genuine laughter, nor can you make your hair stand on end by any palpable sleight-of-hand. But for some of us certain poems, pieces of prose or music bring about this phenomenal manifestation without fail; it is something completely beyond our control, a manifestation that starts in the mind, not on the skin. And for those in doubt, gooseflesh is a reassuring proof that you are still alive.

Words for me have more potency in this respect than music. But others swear that certain bits of opera every time they hear them will melt their limbs and bring them out all bumpy. Boys' voices must be universal manipulators and there's a point in Thomas Tallis's 40-part motet, *Spem in alium*, where I know, inevitably and beyond my rational control, I shall knuckle under. But more often it's poems which have a volatile control over my skin. 'Wild Swans at Coole' by Yeats has claimed me for years (which proves it isn't the unexpected that is all of a sudden overwhelming). Kipling's 'The Path Through the Woods', Ted Hughes's 'Horses', and bits of Gerard Manley Hopkins, Emily Brontë, Francis Thompson, Robert Frost and many others have me in their power, as well as that more tacky poem, 'Cynara', by Ernest Dowson. Flecker is a natural, a dependable gooseflesher, and even bits of Browning can do it. Martin Luther King's 'I have a dream . . .' gets some every time.

In a way they are each emotional clichés – far from being obscure or esoteric – a kind of lingua franca we all share to greater or lesser degrees. Motoring through Wales recently my companion and I pooled our own personal touch-papers and found ourselves in accord; when he started to quote some of the poems, I could almost feel the air in the car becoming ionized. Does this arcane happening take us all in the same way, I wonder: starting on the arms, then the back of the neck, the scalp, the thighs and so on?

There is another preoccupation, not so quirky but of equal intensity, which, though it may not bring out gooseflesh, can make my heart pound and cause an involuntary 'Ohhhh . . .' of disbelief. It comes from having a bee's look at flowers. The impact of colour and design when looking into the heart of a flower through a powerful magnifying glass is mind blowing. Pistil, anther, stigma and filament are a revelation of faultless construction.

When a certain dispirited dejection hangs about a garden, on days when marguerites are stressed from drought or the trees knee-deep in summer, when the bog garden is a steaming poultice and the air as sticky as the flowers on a petunia, walk around peering into the eye of a flower to revive your wilting spirits. Lacecap hydrangeas are miraculous; the spines on robinia, instead of appearing soft, which they are in reality, when magnified are barbs, fiercely red and protective; when looked at closely, Bells of Ireland, green flowers with stems the colour of *vin rosé*, have veins as fine as a spider's web; the heart of a penstemon appears anatomical – not bee country at all; try lightly shaking the black stamen of an overblown crimson poppy for its satiny and erotic showiness.

Looked at through a lens the viola 'Irish Molly' has an open throat with white fringing on the upper palate and a fine black line outlining each petal, just as a glass is edged with salt for a margarita cocktail, and looked at from the back, the purple veins are arranged like whale-boning in a corset. The rose 'Golden Wings' has a dense collection of brittle stamens crafted as intricately as a piece of underwater coral. As for honeysuckles, they aren't flowers at all but the back view of some tropical bird with their tail feathers furled. The bluish-purple solanum seems to be saying 'read my lips' as it sticks out a proboscis in a wickedly salacious way.

Seen close-to, the five maroon blotches and the gaudy stamens of the papery flowers *Cistus ladanifer* (now renamed *C.* x *cyprius*) look like the psychedelic work of a pop-artist. Others have an imperceptible bloom on them of the kind that you find on old and often-laundered linen, and oddly, the petals of some potentillas appear to have the texture of pre-cast concrete. To be truly confounded put your eye to a balloon flower, *Platycodon grandiflorum*: the balloons are as fragile as the membrane of a dragonfly and the flower, when open, seems almost to pulsate from its own vibrant blueness. Once, looking into the heart of the rose 'Francis E. Lester', its half-closed petals still retaining the pinky look which later fades, I found a browsing spider with a body like a blob of mercury and legs so delicate and transparent as to make any Venetian glass-blower throw in the sponge.

When you scrutinize buds rising up the spire of a hollyhock, you'll see how the five segments of each one are covered with hairs finer than gossamer. At the centre of a white double hollyhock, whose flowers are as many-layered as a ballet dancer's tutu, there's a yellow luminosity about its crumpled petals from invisible stamens deep within. Yet when you look into the centre of a red hollyhock the character of the flower is changed entirely by its shadowy-black and veiled heart.

But for sheer wonder, look down the funnel of a foxglove and you might imagine yourself in an extravagant stage set designed by Rex Whistler, where the walls and ceiling are spotted with purple, except where the paint has run, leading to a distant translucent green descent as you pass under peachy ornaments suspended overhead in the most outré and theatrical fashion.

Black is not a colour often found in the garden. '"Faust", the black pansy, has come to pay me its Easter visit,' wrote Colette in one of her many minutely observed essays on flowers. 'Here it is, on my table, only slightly less black than my black velvet jacket. When the sun strikes it, it is imbued with a dusting of constellations, revealing the fact that the reigning principle behind so much blackness is a blue, no purple, no, blue so substantial that it wins our admiration.' The black of pansies is indeed elusive. Along with the black body-colour of auriculas, the opulent blackness of pansies is so hard to describe that it made Colette falter. And here is Proust likening Albertine's hair to black violets: 'For, quite contrarily, every morning the ripple of her hair, for instance, continued to give me the same surprise, as though it were some novelty that I had never seen before. And yet, above the smiling eyes of a girl, what could be more beautiful than that clustering coronet of black violets?'

I know I go on, rather, about looking at a flower through a tiny lens and discovering the intricacy of design and texture, but this particular garden preoccupation is so revealing and shocking that it is worth ten minutes' diversion from the watering. It is also slow; so slow that progressing from flower to flower has the same fascination as when you walk through the countryside rather than drive.

This way of looking at flowers may seem kinky; a distortion of what a garden is about. And in a way I agree. It is a form of homing-in on the infinitesimal instead of looking at the garden as a whole, as a composition with form and atmosphere. At school we used to peer at Shakespeare; shredding his poetry to bits. It was called analysis. I did not want Shakespeare filleted for me as in the abridged editions but neither did I want this form of dissection. En masse the class closed in on every phrase, minutely scrutinizing each word until all sense of cadence had been fragmented long before we had finished the play.

Education is a real killer like this. Before school age children are susceptible to whatever catches their attention. But what on earth do we do to them once they go to school? Instead of throwing down a hundred wonders for children to listen to or look at, pursue or reject, we force them to take up attitudes long before they need until their innate responses and curiosity have long since been eroded. Exams are part of it, this passing through a narrowing funnel which leads to four-hour questionnaires to test a pupil's memory. Those that survive and come out the other side, have done so not because but in spite of education. We squander a child's potential which should be cultivated, not sprayed with a systemic.

It was to avoid this crushing of a child's spirit that we educated our children first, in Thailand, at the local kindergarten and the primary school in the small town where we lived and then, when we moved to Corfu, at the village school. There they went by donkey up the earthy lane leading to the village, through billows of heavily-scented broom in June, or in winter, with hot baked potatoes in their pockets to keep their hands warm, through olive groves where women bent double, wearing full cotton skirts and aprons with large pockets in front, were picking the fruit off the ground.

Our children may have lost out on bunsen burners and becoming streetwise at nine, but they did learn how to tell what wild 'weeds' were eatable, several languages and the legends of Odysseus. Can one truly say which sort of education was the best? Impossible. It only proves that, like gardening, there are no right ways, only alternatives.

The tales of Odysseus' adventures were spell-binding for children, but for me the one chapter which I still find most moving, full of presentiment and overcast with gloom is 'The Book of the Dead' when Circe sends Odysseus to the river of Hell to seek counsel from the prophet Tiresias.

After he had made his libations and sacrifices, and received the predictions for his journey home to Ithaca, Odysseus then called up the

dead. As each soul appeared before him the overpowering sense of grief became increasingly portentous. Reaching out to his mother he cried in despair, 'Why do you avoid me when I try to reach you so that even in Hell we may throw our loving arms around each other's necks and draw cold comfort from our tears?' One by one the dead recalled their intimidating accounts of how they died.

First came the women, the wives and daughters of princes, who told their awesome tales of guile and seduction followed by Odysseus' heroic comrades retelling their deaths in the Trojan War or the fate that befell them on their journeys home. Agamemnon and Patroclus and fleet-footed Achilles who asked Odysseus how he dared come below to the land of Hades 'where the dead live on without their wits as disembodied ghosts'.

As more comrades pressed around him their lamentations increased; they implored Odysseus to tell them of their children, of their fate up there in the sunlit world. These were followed by Minos, son of Zeus, Orion, Tantalus and mighty Heracles, 'his wraith, that is to say, since he himself banquets at ease with the immortal gods and has for consort Hebe of the slim ankles . . .'.

Odysseus lingered on, hoping to meet the men who died even further back in time – such as Theseus – but as he waited the dead multitudes gathered round him with such eerie cries that: 'Sheer panic turned me pale, gripped by the sudden fear that dread Persephone might send me up from Hades's Halls some ghastly monster like the Gorgon's head. I made off quickly to my ship and told my men to embark and loose the hawsers. They climbed in at once and took their seats on the benches, and the current carried her down the River of Ocean, helped by our oars at first and later by a friendly breeze.' So ends 'The Book of the Dead', and with deep sighs of relief the reader moves on to the next chapter, towards the rosy-fingered dawn.

A few minutes from where I live is a market. Three times a week (four in the summer), in the square in front of the eleventh-century castle, there are stalls with enough provender and diversity of goods to supply every human necessity. Salubrity of the flesh and spirit are amply catered for. Besides the usual things such as fish, meat, fruit and cheese, on Saturdays there is a cake stall where customers descend like a flock of sparrows to buy freshly-made cakes from a young woman who has a tireless capacity for baking new models almost every week. If you arrive at the market without having eaten breakfast, and have the stamina, there's a stall selling bacon and eggs or veggie burgers sizzling hot to be eaten on the run. Mops, sweaters, toys and gaudy jewellery, brass bells, antique box Brownies, discarded bowler hats and cosy bedroom slippers like great-grandpapa wore, are laid out tempting every strolling passer-by to reach out for something.

But most persuasively, at arbitrary sites throughout the market, are stalls loaded with plants exuding scent and a sense of glorious verdancy, promising each one of us a colourful summer way beyond our dreams. Particularly in spring.

Then, instead of bringing home what I had set out to buy, I fill my basket with plants. Everything in the market looks far prettier and more tempting than anything to be seen in garden centres, which are becoming more uninviting each year. Near here three, at least, which used to be pleasant nurseries irresistible and helpful, have become as impersonal and unrelated to gardens as hypermarkets are to the kitchen. The junk associated with gardens, which nowadays confronts you on the threshold of a garden centre more interested in plastic furniture and pesticides than in the serious business of horticulture, is so naff that I turn away in despair and depend on the market stalls instead.

This spring I fell for the *Violaceae* family, though it was a close thing with the equally enchanting clan of pinks. Having left small holes between the bricks and cobbles in the courtyard, I am filling them with thyme and violas from the market; at the foot of climbers against the wall I'm keeping to cream, yellow, orange and blue campanulas, violas and pansies.

Pansies look like cats with velvet faces, but as they far exceed the feline inhabitants in our gardens, we barely stop to think about them. For years we have been growing pansies, often not bothering to consider whether they are pansies or violas or even violettas. Not that it matters. To many of us, dead set on enhancing our gardens whatever their name, *Violaceae* are the most compliant flowers, with their benevolent life style and long-flowering habits. By having such motley tones they clamour to be used overflowing from a huddle of pots, or like embroidery joining plant to plant in a flowerbed. Though in my garden the pansies do better in shade, when seen suddenly in a slipstream of sunlight the flowers make boundaries like imperial silk where the light catches their petals.

Whichever name you give them, *Violaceae* portray an absolute distillation of spring. In the cool and fragile weeks of April sweet violets lurk on banks, their damp redolence rivalling that of primroses for sighs and nostalgia; in cottage gardens violas and pansies are as quintessential as the hollyhock, nor should the species viola be underrated as a garden flower just because of its diminutive size. They're good survivors, hardy, and agreeable to being planted in humble sites where they fill cracks and corners with dogged stamina.

Once, at the end of the nineteenth century, there was a 'Viola Conference' to make sure that violettas toed the line. In the finely honed distinction between the three – pansy, viola and violetta – it was imperative to note that the smaller plants, the violettas, don't have rays on their petals – lines as fine as eyelashes radiating from the centre – but they do have the clumpy growth of violas and a delicious vanillary smell reminiscent of teatime and sponge cakes. In fact, our only scented species in these islands is the sweet violet, *Viola odorata*, with a scent esteemed above all others by some connoisseurs of our wild flowers. But never inhale too long or too deeply. Perversely, the violet has an inbuilt chemical which numbs our olfactory sensibilities even as we sniff.

Love for pansies has been constant; going back to long before the

Viola canadensis.

Viola odorata var praecox.

Viola cornuta (*Horned Pansy*).

Viola Munbyana (*Algerian Violet*).

1830s when they were added to the tulip, pink and auricula as the florists' favourite flowers. (Unbelievably they were superseded by the dahlia. 'Dahlia mania' was rife by the 1840s.) At that time the pansy was without its familiar blotches which make it so distinctive nowadays, the flower had merely a few dark lines; not until the lines began to merge one into the other did pansies have the open-faced naïvety, expressing each flower's individual persona.

Pansies have been the inspiration for poetry, art and music; for fabric design, wallpaper and tombstones. Clutched to bosoms, the highly scented, glossy-leafed and double-petalled Parma violets had a wealth of cloying potency. In cookery their petals were added to chicken or meat dishes or turned into syrup, tea and violet ice cream. In London there are certain confectionery shops famous for their violet-centred chocolates decorated with crystallized flowers, so sought-after that people come from miles away intent on easing their craving for these gooey-centred sweets. A 'Violet Tea' was recommended as 'a pretty idea' in *Cassell's Household Guide*, published in 1911, when cakes were made to match the flowers on the table. Icing the colour of violets was embellished with a cluster of crystallized flowers, their stalks made from strips of angelica.

Used like blotting paper the flowers were strewn on the floors of cottage, manor or church to absorb and disperse the musty smell of damp. In the countryside violets were gathered on Mothering Sunday; in more urban settings it was fashionable to wear a bunch pinned to a muff, and for the fastidious gentleman a pansy in the buttonhole might upstage a rose.

With their implied virtue of modesty and innocence, violets regularly turned up on valentines; they were embroidered on hankies or waistcoats and devout ladies still cross-stitch them onto hassocks. Printed on tea towels they are assumed to lure innumerable visitors walking through National Trust shops on their way out of houses and

46

gardens. Lovelorn swains, myopic from passion, have gone as far as to describe their beloved's eyes as the colour of violets.

In paintings, tapestries, triptychs or murals violets have appeared as minor decorations or as linking colours binding the central subject to the design. Two exquisite colour plates on sixteenth-century documents that record the grants of arms from Robert Cooke, Clarenceux, to Henry Stanley of Sutton Bonnington, Nottingham and to George Toke of Worcester, have borders of flowers. The first includes a violet, the second a few pansies. In heraldry two French families, the Villy and the Vaultier *dit* Beauregard, used violets in their coats of arms, as did the Van Groenendyk family in Holland.

A thousand years or so before John Gerard's *Herball* appeared at the end of the sixteenth century and long before he planted violets in his own garden at Holborn where he grew 'all manner of strange trees, herbes, rootes, plants, flowers, and other such rare things', Queen Radegonde of France was growing violets. When she founded a nunnery at Poitiers, Bishop Fortunatus sent her some scented plants, among them violets. And imagine how, in the last century, the sight of violets grown to supply the famous perfume distilleries of Grasse spread like a ruffled sea of implausible hue over twelve hundred acres of the aptly named Côte d'Azur.

The artist Pierre-Joseph Redouté, renowned for immortalizing the Empress Josephine's collection of roses, had among his paintings of favourite flowers a portrait of *La Pensée*, the wild pansy, heartsease, and a painting, *Bouquet de Pensées*, in which the 'honey guides' (those little lines radiating from the centre which head visiting bees in the right direction) on each flower are as finely delineated as the antennae of a butterfly; the orange eye, the blotches, the furled buds among reflexed leaves, are of such meticulous precision you can sense their dewy freshness. A lesser-known artist than Redouté, or Dürer with his famed drawing of violets, is a painter with the resounding name of Joshua

Reynolds Gascoigne Gwatkin, from Potterne near Devizes, who painted heartsease, sweet and marsh violets and the humorous *Viola contempta*, with minute accuracy. As he only started painting after a career in the Royal Wilts Yeomanry, while having an unflagging enthusiasm for hunting and shooting, it adds a certain piquancy when looking at his tender portraits of such reticent flowers.

These quiet flowers may be world famous, symbolic for such diverse reasons as politics or morality, but in Spain it is their more mundane association that sets my pulse racing. In Madrid there's a shop called 'Violetta' given over to every aspect imaginable which has to do with violets. Even the wrapping paper, ribbon and bills are that colour.

William Robinson, the great gardening guru born in 1838, whose pen was often dipped in acid when writing about what people did to their gardens, became almost lyrical over the viola: 'some of which are among the most beautiful ornaments which bedeck the alpine turf.' And: 'From the Violet our world of wild flowers derives wondrous beauty and delicate fragrance; no family has given us anything more precious than the garden Pansies.' Many gardeners will say amen to that.

D. H. Lawrence, in his collection of poems *Pansies*, which he wanted to be read as casual thoughts, as *pensées* that rang true at some moments but were irrelevant at others, has a certain detached pungency when he says: 'flowers, to my thinking, are not merely pretty-pretty. They have in their fragrance an earthiness of the humus and the corruptive earth from which they spring. And pansies, in their streaked faces, have a look of many things besides heartsease.' True. I have long been aware of the liquid manure that goes to make a peach.

Certainly Lawrence would not have approved of pansies grown for exhibition. By the 1850s the show and fancy pansies had erupted into monsters of ostentatious splendour with their swollen heads described chillingly in the judges' language of specific assessment as: 'self, mottled, suffused, striped or margined but most important of all it should possess no ray nor blotch.'

No ray? No blotch? Horrors! Strictures so forthright as to make any violet shrink. Like show dogs with their mutilated tails and ears, these exhibition and fancy pansies had come so far from their innocent origins

that, for the purpose of exhibition, some had to wear cardboard collars. Worse still, there came a time when the head of the pansy was severed to facilitate its being lined up for easy scrutiny on a board when not a vestige of deviant behaviour was allowed to impair its circular precision, judged with a pair of compasses.

Forced, coaxed, hybridized, measured and anthropomorphized, the flower has become inextricably bound into all our conceptions of sweetness and harmony. However bad-tempered, there would be few of us who could stamp on a pansy and not wince on behalf of a cat.

Spring is notoriously fickle. We may have three or four weeks of drought followed by days of rain. Rain to which we have looked forward so hopefully always turns out to be not so pleasant as the rain to which we had been looking forward.

For one thing walking on sodden ground at this time of year inevitably means crushing underfoot the small piercing leaves of bulbs. As you tread unwittingly on them they give an ominous crunch like that of a snail going to its death. Spring is a season for clearing up after winter; when things in the garden move in spurts and bounds, and when every year I'm fooled by iris leaves: appearing dead, I give them a pull, only to find they are still attached to the corm. Spring brings days when streamers of white clouds pass continually across the sky, when the fussing of birds surrounds us in the garden and the progress of speedwell threading through grass is as convoluted as voices singing the office of compline.

It is the season when there's an urgency in the air as the residual breath of winter finally evaporates. And it is now I want auriculas – flowers which are an antidote to all this prettiness, to so much blue and yellow; to the tenderness of beech leaves as moist and crinkled as a baby's palm; to nature's effusive charm and the restless feeling, that whatever I'm doing, I could be doing something else.

Auriculas are flowers of such impeccable beauty that they never seem to have sprung from anything as elemental as earth. What are they? Such precision in spring cannot have evolved alongside all the thrusting, sexy, lushness of disruptive nature? Immaculate; their conception took place far from the crude stench of manure.

Actually *Primula auricula* have been lurking for centuries in crevasses and rocky fissures of the Alps and Pyrenees, and what we have now are the results of numerous crosses between plants first made hundreds of years ago by Flemish weavers fleeing to Britain from religious persecution. Willingly we should mentally genuflect to those many florists since then who, with besotted devotion, have given us sophisticated flowers of such recherché colours as amaranth, bronze, ecru or deep Tyrian purple.

Florists were nothing like those of today who supply us with pot plants, carnations and maidenhair wrapped up in cellophane; they were men, mostly in the north of England, who cultivated a particular group of flowers with single-minded zeal to breed plants to an exacting standard. The pink, tulip, anemone and ranunculus; the hyacinth, carnation, polyanthus and the auricula were among the classic list of florists' flowers whose every variation of striped, spotted or double form was scrupulously cultivated by their devotees. The nomenclature of auriculas evolved, defining alpine from show; self, fancy or edged; farina and meal, which came from the extraordinary and much prized frosted appearance on the leaf and flower of show auriculas.

Where else could we find such enigmatic colours as those of rosy-violet auriculas with topaz throats, or others all golden-petalled with white lambent eyes? Some are the opaque green of a northern sea, or swarthy crimson with a lightness of spangling silver, others may be turbid purple with pale-lime centres; feathered russet edged with verdigris, or toxic yellow and raw silk. And some are the brownish-mauve of a rotting Victoria plum.

But here's the problem: where do you site these works of art with their sturdy stems, many of which have coarse leaves covered with a mealy whiteness − proof of the flower's chastity − and designed with anatomical draughtsmanship so refined as to require rarified air and pure light and no turbulence? Not among commoners, surely? Nor yet among aristocrats − even though there is a certain hubris about their bearing; nor can they be set against grandeur, or in some cute little niche. In the eighteenth century there were auricula 'theatres', ornate and lamplit, with mirrors and backcloths of black velvet. Somehow that doesn't answer my question; the contrived stage wouldn't be my choice.

Unlike most flowers, auriculas are rigid, their deportment unyielding. Without movement, they cannot merge as other flowers do, being neither flimsy, sinuous, drooping nor pliable, and never, never will they stir to the wind. Rose, pansy or harebell − even a tulip with reflexed petals and slightly scrolled leaves − have lines which flow. But not the

auricula. No, the flowers must be sited at eye level, as close-to as a
breath when it mists a glass. Every frill and tuck, every stripe and
mottle, each variation of texture from velour to shantung, the deep-sea
jade piping, the snow-white hemming, the grey bloom of the mealy
border must be minutely observed.

I give up. I swoon for them – almost go goosefleshy – but admit
defeat. The truth is that the flower is an artifact: a plant far removed
from the hurly-burly of gardens in spring.

CHAPTER IV

A GROUND PLOT FOR THE MIND
France

'I SHALL RETURN WITH THE VIOLETS IN SPRING.' These romantic words were spoken by Napoleon before he was exiled to Elba. After the débâcle of Waterloo and his death some years later on St Helena, he was found to be carrying a locket containing violets taken from Josephine's grave. She had worn violets on her wedding day and had been presented by the emperor with a bunch on each anniversary and during his exile Napoleon's loyal supporters wore bunches of violets as symbols of their constancy.

Such flowery fidelity has not much to do with the way we do things today. Even in France, romance is not one of the ingredients universally found in gardens. But privacy is. Researching for a book, *The Secret Gardens of France*, I met gardeners with strong feelings, both passionate and committed, for their own very personal retreats, not indoors where you might look for solitude, but outside, under the trees. Both the gardens and their owners made such an impression on me that I can't shake free of their fascination. Even now, making a new garden, I'm still partially under the spell of Gallic sensibilities as I try to restrain my instinct for floral chaos.

Our fairly sweeping impressions of what the French do to their gardens, gathered from glimpses as we drive through the countryside,

have nothing to do with the reality. What goes on behind walls is a revelation. And though some French gardeners regularly travel to Britain, it becomes very apparent when talking to them that their ideas have germinated, not in English, but in French soil.

I have succumbed to what they do with the shears: to the ease with which they guillotine trees, lining them up into aisles of white blossom; to their ability to trepan shrubs into rows of uniform subjects; and to their instinct to keep nature at bay with none of the soul-searching that the American writer, Michael Pollan, in his book *Second Nature*, goes in for. 'Once you accept the landscape as a moral and spiritual space, ornamental gardening becomes problematic. For how can one presume to remake God's landscape? It is one thing to cultivate the earth for our sustenance – the Bible speaks of that – but to do so for aesthetic reasons has until very recently struck Americans as frivolous, or worse.'

But what if you don't accept the landscape as a moral and spiritual space? Having none of those hang-ups, long ago the French laid hold of their countryside and pounded, falsified, cajoled, uprooted, irrigated, threatened and dramatized it until they had created controlled vistas on a gargantuan scale. And this same bias on a far smaller scale has filtered down through the centuries and can still be found in the very private, very sequestered plots belonging to French gardeners.

Born with the automaton set to PRUNE, very sensibly they have none of the American's anguish. As one lady said apropos her attempt to make a bit of wild garden: 'Well me, I'm French! I don't have that feeling naturally. I love organizing plants – the roses – but how I should like to disorganize!' And so it has been for centuries. Russell Page, who designed gardens for the grand and rich owners of *châteaux*, considered that the French accepted designs and materials only if they conformed to French style, and that they only sought plants which provided 'the form logically required'. Logically required? That sort of philosophy would have knocked on the head most of our English gardens at one fell blow.

Anyone can make a tidy garden: a central lawn, mown regularly, a few trees dotted about, a border of flowers along the boundaries and, *voilà*, it is done. On both sides of the English channel this sort of garden is ubiquitous. It requires neither inspiration nor flair, nor does it uplift our spirits or reveal an iota of creativity from the owner. All it shows is a hackneyed template for neatness and order, which to maintain is as deadly predictable as washing the car each Saturday. But that kind of discipline is not what I am talking about. The French instinct for control is something quite different. And I long to have it. Not for the sake of the attribute itself, far from it, but for the kind of garden it leads to.

Their way with the pruning knife is a revelation. Used to dealing with vines, the French are merciless; their espaliers flanking gravel paths with arms outstretched in amiable conviviality, through which are glimpses of vegetables and peonies, are masterpieces of subordination. Their courtyards filled with variegations of textures and greenness from box, rosemary or lavender cut into scrupulous spheres without a hair out of place; their hornbeam hedges of such unerring precision you feel, as you walk between them, the comfort of straight lines; and the way they chasten trees, pollarding them into submission until in winter their ancient branches form contortions of monstrous beauty, all combine to create a form of garden tradition impossible to resist.

Though such stiff-necked gardens are as far away as you can get from going weak-kneed over turbulent roses, they do form an almost consummate sense of repose. With cerebral application the French amputate their plants to the bare bones, making an unobtrusive background for any flowers which they have chosen with Gallic logic to include. 'I must snip, clip and cut!' cried one gardener looking at her lilac. 'I cut it to death. And what happened? It grew magnificent flowers with no leaves!' The result was fabulous. Had I had the chance, and been intrepid enough, to show her our wild garden, I would have had to steel myself for her indrawn breath and shocked reaction to such

Anglo-Saxon impropriety, undisciplined and rash.

'One has to put in flowers,' another French lady grudgingly admitted, 'but not too many.' I say hallelujah to that qualification. We were walking through her garden as full of rocks, boulders, stone walls and trees as of flowers. If, according to John Ruskin, 'mountains are the beginning and the end of all natural scenery', for me trees are the beginning and the end of all gardens. And here, with a watchful sense of discrimination, the owner had restricted herself to only those trees and flowers which worked for her – mimosas, pines, abutilons, rock roses, ceanothus, euphorbia and straggling clematis binding the garden together with random tacking stitches.

It is this incisive self-restraint, these subjugated shrubs, their *potagers*, the flowers grown for the house; their gravel paths, box edgings, cordons, arches, and trees standing in methodical regularity among red cabbages and beets, that I found in gardener after gardener. Nowhere did I come across people who, with insatiable longings to home-in on the nearest garden centre, greedily swept up everything on the brink of flowering. Except for a bedding-plant fanatic in one place and a rosy megalomaniac in another – each of whom indulged to such excess that their gardens were a total-immersion experience of exquisite madness – the gardeners I met showed not a vestige of impetuous avarice. And but for one gardener, who counted her agapanthus every night to make sure none had been stolen, French gardeners were so laid back about man-made as well as natural disasters that they gave an impression of serenity both enviable and difficult to emulate. Their acceptance of climatic boundaries (much more critical than in England) seemed total. As a philosophy towards gardening it was an eye-opener, and the more gardens I visited the more I respected their tolerant acquiescence – as well as their lust for decapitation.

My companions on the quest for French gardens were my daughter Tamsin and her six-month-old daughter Cassandra, whose tendency to

rip to pieces paper tablecloths as we waited for our meal in the more humble establishments created either good-humoured amusement or withering looks from the peroxided *madame*.

I wanted to call my book on French gardens *The Melancholy Voice of Frogs*, in deference to Alphonse de Lamartine whose pastoral poetry is so poignant, but I suppose it might have been misconstrued.

Remembering his childhood in Burgundy, Lamartine writes sadly of how he half imagines he still hears 'the sweet and melancholy voices of the little frogs that sing on summer evenings'. Wistfully he recalls the rustic bench where his father sat, the upturned ploughshares where the shepherds rested, or how his mother, with a slight sigh, left the house.

Michael and I went to look through the locked gates of the garden about which he wrote: 'in this poor enclosure, long since deserted, emptied by death; in these alleys overrun by weeds, by moss, and the pinks from the beds under those old trunks drained of sap, but not of souvenirs – on this unraked sand, my eye still seeks the footprints of my mother, of my sisters, old friends, old servants of the family, and I go and sit under the fence opposite the house, which is buried year by year deeper under the ivy, beneath the rays of the setting sun to the hum of insects, the sound of the lizards on the old wall, whom I seem to recognize as old garden guests, and to whom it seems I might gossip about old times.'

This piece of prose should have taken centre-stage in my book on French gardens. *The Melancholy Voice of Frogs* would have been a salutation to a man who could write of his childhood garden in a voice that croons with such moving sonority.

Burgundy is a good place for gardens, whether they are well-concealed country ones, courtly *potagers* or seventeenth-century walled sanctuaries of magnificent decrepitude. And it's in this region in particular that it's common to see in winter the handsome and rectangular houses belonging to hotelier or farmer where the tendrils of a leafless Virginia creeper, dividing and subdividing into fragmentary threads, enclose the building like a caul. Here, too, among the Charollais cows, the Romanesque churches and poplar trees whose leaves in April are the colour of bruised nectarines, gardeners revealed their thoughts on some gardening detail.

One pointed out how few structures the French use in their gardens. Another spoke with a quiet passion about how her garden was only that of an amateur but – '*Je l'adore! J'y passe ma vie*. I spend all of my life here – it's my good fortune to work out-of-doors!' One showed us how a small oval surround, originally intended as a base for a sundial but now filled up with water, made 'an eye that reflects a fragment of the sky.' Another stated simply: 'I'm completely cuckoo about roses!' And one gardener said: 'I like empty pots in my garden. You can wonder what to put in them.' Looking at them, the warm pink of Elastoplast rather than the strident colour of new bricks, she added: 'It's like waiting at a concert hall for the music to start.'

In 1577 a book was published called *The Gardener's Labyrinth*. In it, the author Thomas Hill describes a garden as a 'ground plot for the mind', and presents his theory on when to plant seeds; those 'of the tender herbs committed to the earth in an apt time, and the moon in her first quarter, do the speedier shoot up, being specially sown after showers of raine, on sunny and warme places . . .'.

More than four hundred years later we came across the same association between the moon and planting when Tamsin and I met Maurice Blanc. Maurice and Annie Blanc, parents of Raymond Blanc, the proprietor of the hotel and restaurant *Le Manoir aux Quat' Saisons* in Oxfordshire, live in one of the most lovely regions of France, the Doubs.

Here, outside the university town of Besançon, is where the Blancs have a small *potager* surrounding their house. As *potagers* are as characteristic of France as geraniums in terracotta pots, and have been going for a good many millennia, it was a relief to be shown one on a digestible scale in contrast to the famous ones, such as that at Villandry. But first we had lunch. This was a relaxed and protracted affair lasting four hours, interspersed by nursery rhymes which Madame Blanc sang to amuse Cassandra.

We began with asparagus, tomatoes and mayonnaise, followed by prosciutto, ham, and Madame Blanc's pickled chanterelles gathered from the nearby woods; young guinea fowl, their own chicory and haricot beans, followed by cheese from the neighbouring farm and the lightest of classic French puddings – *îles flottantes*. Not until we had drunk our coffee did Monsieur Blanc explain how he gardens *avec la lune*.

To plant in rhythm to the moon's progress is no longer a common practice, yet judging by the fecundity of Maurice Blanc's garden, nourished not by chemical fertilizers but by seaweed, rotted rabbit manure and soil from the forest, the moon has a lot going for it when it comes to putting seeds into the earth. *'On sème les légumes en vieille lune, et on sème les fleurs en jeune lune.'* He never alters the pattern: vegetables are sown when the moon is old, flowers when it is young and nothing goes in, whatever the weather, before the fifteenth of May.

Annie and Maurice Blanc belong to a dying breed: they are traditionalists and have no patience with the ever-growing trend towards short cuts and fast food. The result was that everything we ate, grown in their garden, tasted strongly of itself. Before we left, Monsieur Blanc rather forlornly remarked how the present generation no longer make gardens – by which he meant kitchen gardens – so the fresh, gutsy taste of vegetables is being lost forever. He put out his hands and made that familiar French shrug, body language which is far more eloquent than words: *'C'est dommage.'*

The variety of gardens we visited in France was so disparate that it is hard to say this or that one was typical. Early one morning, in a village in the Loire, we looked at a diminutive example of what Russell Page describes as a 'formal pattern laid out like a carpet', a pattern that has been around since the sixteenth century, extending 'the formalities of the salon into the open air'. Passing through a gateway set in a lofty wall, it was impossible not to salute all those dead-pan pessimists who with their sarcastic aphorisms had forewarned me about French gardens: '*What* French gardens?' Was this an example of what they had been on about? Yet its charm lay in restraint; in intimacy, seclusion and the owners' quiet love for their garden. If the geometric beds filled with alternating pink, red and cream begonias were the French cliché *par excellence*, then here in low-gear gardening was the epitome of France.

But the joke was on us. When our host took us indoors, we stepped into a world of piquant extremes. The worldliness and taste inside obliterated the unpretentious French banality outside. Garden and interior were delightfully out of kilter. In a room lined from floor to ceiling with black felt was a collection of the work of Sonia Delaunay – a Russian pioneer of abstract painting who died in 1974. As we sat in semi-darkness drinking pink champagne and eating nuts from a porcelain dish said to have been moulded on the breast of Marie Antoinette (our host explained how the nipple used to be pink before the manufacturers lost their nerve and left it white), we had time to relish the unlikeliness of the occasion.

From within the darkened room was a view across the lane where a weeping willow leant over a stream. The morning light on the water made the sparkling surface mobile and if a long-skirted lady pushing a high-wheeled pram had walked by at that moment, I couldn't have been more surprised than I was already at the way we were spending our morning. When we finally left such generous hospitality it was with a keen appreciation of the incongruity of the room, the paintings and the garden.

One day, after travelling through tracts of the wild upland regions of the Cantal where there was a fête of *transhumants* going on, including a *passage des troupeaux et des attelages traditionels* followed by a *repas Montagnard*, a dinner-dance, and a cow as first prize at the tombola, Tamsin and I reluctantly resisted the temptation to linger but

continued south, dropping height towards the fat lands of tourism in Provence. Not far from Arles is a *mas*, the southern name for a house or farm. The house was a dream, a Renaissance masterpiece with the sort of proportions which make you involuntarily sigh. The walls of the house were the pallid gold of autumn sunlight, the shutters the colour of sloes bleached almost to dust. Beneath these, running the length of the house, were pale pink trusses of voluptuous semi-double roses mingled with white valerian and blue plumbago. It was a sight to die for.

Lolling roses, fussily embroidered by single pink geraniums, spilt out of stone troughs placed in the middle ground against a black backdrop of yews cut into rising pyramids of immaculate geometry. Ancient irrigation channels crossed the garden, rather like those in Moghul enclosures except these were more decorative, with curlicues where one channel crossed another. A short avenue of cypress trees led to a deep well; a path, flanked by agapanthus, led to a large stone pot filled with senecios and pinky-white geraniums, and nearby lavender bushes, four foot high, five foot in diameter, appeared to shimmer like some fabulous Fabergé ornament from the quivering wings of thousands of turquoise-striped damsel flies which hid every flower from sight. Further away a colonnade of stone pillars covered with vines led to a stone bridge and a patch of wilderness full of bamboos where the boundary hedge made of bay formed a border behind a flounce of pink and white oleanders. Far across the field were willows, Judas and loquat trees, their fruit just turning yellow, and a grove of olives.

As I write now, in an English July, I think of that late May garden. How at this time of year it will be surrounded by burnt-up grass on the flat land beyond the *mas* and how the chestnuts, pines and planes will cast deep black shadows in the early morning and late evening. 'The English have a sensitivity towards their gardens that we don't have,' I remember one French gardener telling me. Ah, you must be wrong. It can't be so. Thinking of the beauty, the symmetry, the roses and

geraniums, the flawless balance between plant and stone, I know that all my preconceptions about gardening on the other side of the Channel can be proved wrong in an instant by walking through that Provençal garden.

Courtyards, those enclosures we hanker for, belong to the south. They exist in Britain, but not as frequently as in those countries bordering the Mediterranean. In France we visited many. Some imposing and severe, so bereft of spontaneous foliage that they failed in every way to make the place vibrant. Others, though still under the control of the shears, had a miraculous harmony between the stones, steps, formal box outlines and spherical bay where a leaning mulberry or a contorted olive tree added such shadowy atmosphere it was impossible not to sit on the stone seat placed there to tempt you to linger. Other courtyards were cluttered: the charm of pots rising in tiers, standing at angles, herded into corners, are so germane to the south that anyone from Britain may wonder momentarily how they had the nerve to try it on at home.

In my back garden I have a courtyard enclosed by an immensely high dry-stone wall on one side and the L-shape of the house on two others; it is utterly private, sheltered and hot. I am trying to decide what plants to ration myself to so that I don't entirely screen the soothing grey of the south-facing wall which must have stood there for several hundred years.

Ceanothus and the rose 'Maigold' went in together. Their colours of blue and orange are a combination I fall for every time. Clematis, solanum and honeysuckle are there too, with violets – yellow and white and as many blue ones as I can lay my hands on – at their feet. But I have to be fairly mingy about my planting; the yard is only about twelve feet across. In place of the pre-cast concrete slabs and the raised bed along the wall of the courtyard, which were there, I've had a floor laid of cobbles, old tiles and bricks, with large iron cauldrons (which were once used for the laundry but now are found abandoned in the fields around here), full of climbers and floppy flowers.

In spring the expression of the courtyard changes when tulips, striped, double, reflexed or frilly-edged and smudgy, stand upright in these rusting boilers. Rust is an irresistible colour; pink tulips and rust, blue petunias and rust make such a delectable alliance that any artist would go potty. I never understand why people throw up their hands at the first sight of rust. I know it's corrosive – but so are prejudices – and oxidized iron is one of the great garden bonuses, whether on overhead pergolas or long-abandoned gate hinges or milking pails used as flowerpots. The colour blends with every flower, even magenta in small clashing flecks about the garden.

And there are pots. Chalky terracotta ones which come from Greece and shatter in the frost if I forget to bring them in; gaudy orange clay crocks I've painted blue, earthenware pitchers, and a huge-bellied vessel from a town in the Périgord, so handsome I leave it unplanted.

'One thing is certain – that when one disappears – that day the garden will be over.' These words were said to me by a Frenchwoman as we stood together looking out over the descending levels of her garden towards a grey sea under a restless sky full of shredded clouds. The garden had been made with the single-minded devotion that overwhelms some gardeners to make such personal places; those sober words, spoken in that setting, were pitiless.

The meaning is inescapable: a garden is ephemeral. And such a terse verdict is the quintessence of gardening: a garden perishes. Nowhere is this more apparent than when the gardener dies; however painstakingly future gardeners with sensitive expertise try to maintain or to recreate the original, some essence, intangible and elusive, is lost forever. What comes after will be different. It may be beautiful, it may appear as an exact replica, but the garden has lost that original thrust; the guiding numen is missing.

When I left the garden which my husband Michael and I had made over ten years, I knew it was finished. Whoever came after would bring their own history, their conditioning and different values, and it was futile to imagine otherwise. Nor did I expect the garden to be perpetuated. The way we had made it was unique to us: to our ignorance, buoyancy, instinct, contriving and floundering, and under no circumstances when I moved elsewhere did I expect the garden to remain petrified in the form we had made it.

This truth is so profound one knows it by not knowing. It requires neither rational thought nor interpretation. (For us the act of shared gardening, not the garden, was what had mattered.) And on that basis whoever came after would bring their own speculative impedimenta – as we had done with ours. There were times as I gardened that I felt taken over: it was not I who was gardening but rather I was being 'gardened'. So that the Frenchwoman's words, 'when one disappears – that day the garden will be over,' chilled my heart with its brutal truth.

What Michael and I had made together had been *then*. Nothing could be what it had been; the only thing was not to look back but to move on into another area; to make something unimpeded by what Michael and I had done. And that's where France comes in. Being under its spell, unable to shake off its presiding power even if I wanted to, I feel at present I am at ease, lying at anchor in the lee of French gardens.

CHAPTER V

THE PERSUASIVE OLEANDER
Summer

A GIRAFFE, WHEN SUDDENLY RAISING ITS HEAD, DOES not black out. Its cardiovascular system is a neat arrangement of eight feet or so of carotid artery. With twice our blood pressure, regardless of its head position, even when it lifts it from drinking, a giraffe's intricate valve system prevents this elegant creature from keeling over. Oh my! Oh my! I think of him browsing in East Africa high among the buds and fruit with his probing lips and long tongue encircling the leaves. My thoughts veer towards other browsers – the elephant. A six-ton colossus, the stuff of fantasy, who also feeds by reaching into lofty regions with a nose so perfectly articulated he devours almost half a ton of greenery a day.

By August when the long days of summer have brought a weariness for colour, when the pyrotechnics gallivanting through the borders are on the decline, I remember Africa. I ponder on the slender giraffe. That miraculous neck. Evolved through centuries: *a complex vascular system to keep a giraffe from swooning.*

When the season has reached its zenith, the garden slumps; when numerous lay-offs have taken place and a certain floral fatigue threatens to overwhelm the garden, we know, that once the yellow has gone out of green and been replaced by dark verdancy, our garden has passed the season of freshness. (Someone once told me that carnations would last

longer – should you want them to – standing in lemonade, which opened up all sorts of possibilities for prolonging life. For instance, would madonna lilies remain immaculate in Liebfraumilch?)

Some of my first memories of gardens are transfixed forever among the barbarian days of summer when my cousin and I would dress up and wander from morning till dusk through the garden in a world of make-believe. We would choose our costumes from a collection of long-forsaken clothes: undergarments of fine cotton with embroidered trimming on petticoats, and bloomers reaching to our knees; lawn blouses, high-necked with countless buttons, and muslin skirts with waists so small we neglected the top hook; sashes, masks, reticules, muffs and an endless choice of ostrich feathers which kept shedding bits wherever we walked. Around our shoulders we draped Chinese shawls of exquisite embroidery or mouldering bits of fur once used for collars on some sumptuous cloak.

There were mittens, made for ladies with fingers as slim as agapanthus stems, which reached right up our arms, and hats of extravagant splendour festooned with ribbons, flowers and glossy cherries – but most wonderful were the fans. We used them as carelessly as a child wields a plastic gun. Their ivory ribs opened to reveal coquettish black lace or painted scenes of eighteenth-century figures seen against willows. One I particularly remember was of ivory-coloured silk surmounted by downy feathers, but my favourite was of such fine yellow silk it had almost rotted away; it had a flower on the side, a cream peony – or was it a rose? The fans lay in narrow boxes lined with pink or ivory satin.

My cousin Judith and I drifted through the garden leaving a waft of mothballs wherever we went, careless of the long fringing on the shawls catching at leaves and roses as we acted out our parts as princesses or danced in imitation of Isadora Duncan in some enchanted land where it never rained. The garden was our theatre: the flowers and butterflies, the lawn, paths, the seats and secret places made an imaginary set which held us captive for hours. There was one particular tree, a huge greengage, under whose branches we sprawled. In retrospect the tree always seemed loaded with fruit as smooth as stones, which we ate till the juice ran down to our elbows. By twilight we had become so mesmerized by the characters we played that we were reluctant to come

indoors, to break the spell and forsake the garden where the light slowly seeped away until only white roses appeared luminous, and bats flitted through the growing dusk.

In winter we used to dress up too, but it never had the magical quality of sauntering through a garden on summer days making up stories as we went among the scents and shadows lying across the lawn which, miraculously, always seemed to have just been mown.

Summer is a time of the year when I grieve for elms, remembering how those huge vegetative trees, which had been with us for eight thousand years, hollowed out the sky. Stricken by Dutch elm disease – which doesn't mean that every tree was a Dutch elm, but just that the fungus had been identified in Holland in 1919. The new strain that appeared in America and Canada in the 1960s was a far more virulent type than the earlier one. The fungus, which is like a yeast in the sap obstructing the flow of nutriments, killed 400,000 trees a year. By 1974 the malady had been four years in Britain and already 4.5 million of our elms had succumbed.

Dutch elm disease became an epidemic on a disastrous scale; bark-beetles spread the fungus with a malignant effectiveness, and where there were dense distributions of the tree, it struck with lethal devastation. Although resistance to the scourge varied according to the species and to the location of the trees, no trees were immune; even the Chinese elm which had been thought to be safe perished. *Ulmus americana* seems to have been very prone, and attempts were made in some parts of America to isolate those trees suffering from the fungus. In the US National Arboretum work was carried out to try to discover a hybrid resistant to the disease. And though elms may eventually return, and even if the young suckers rising now from the base of infected elms successfully mature, already a whole generation of people will have grown up since the trees stood about our landscape.

Those who have never seen the familiar outline of English elms, with their tumbling foliage falling in billowing folds, are to be pitied. Their silhouettes, whether in winter or in summer, were monumental; they could never be confused with others in the family, such as wych elm with its much more rounded profile. And for how much longer will craftsmen be able to work the wood from a dwindling legacy of elms? Trees which in maturity reached about a hundred-and-twenty feet; their wood, of

such durable quality it could withstand water, had a grain so twisted it could never be cleft. But for generations it was used for the hubs of cartwheels, in water mills, for barge bottoms, wheelbarrows, weatherboarding and for coffins; and more domestically for chair seats, egg cups, bellows, bowls, bakers' troughs and washing dollies.

The death of elms is as cataclysmic to a landscape as the loss of olive trees would be to Italy. Anyone young, reading the poetry of Edward Thomas now, cannot empathize with his frequent imagery of elms. Oaks and beeches are magnificent, but elms, seen standing along the hedgerows, are now only to be found in paintings.

Those Victorian and Edwardian paintings of domestic countryside and gardens transcend reality: evocatively, sentimentally and nostalgically. When the sun slopes across the garden and the light on roses is like a held breath, that is the time when artists petrified the instant in watercolours. Through them we inhabit a world of wishful thinking; when the days were sunny; when gardens full of hollyhocks and bowers of roses festooned the porches of thatched cottages secure against the rain.

Lovely Helen, George and Ernest protecting us from the nastiness of *Lark Rise to Candleford* and all that stuff. Poverty is banished; dilapidation, squalor and mud are expunged. Not a whiff of the privy springs from the pictures of Helen Allingham to whom we are indebted for her observant recording of cottages long before developers got their hands on the plumbing. George Samuel Elgood, Ernest Arthur Rowe, Beatrice Parsons and Alfred Parsons (not related), are among so many who painted pictures of summer plenitude. And behind the espaliers in their paintings, behind the ranks of standard roses and deep borders, bent double behind the topiary, stand invisible squads of gardeners. I do not knock them – these paintings. I adore them, finding in their scenes a celestial fairyland whose sweetness trickles through the joints of my mind in the tawdry days of summer.

The painters portrayed their view of pastoral Elysium. Gardeners do the same. Searching for escape they set out to create serenity or retreat, spectacle or illusion. For my part ideas have got no further than my head.

> *Make me a willow cabin at your gate,*
> *And call upon my soul within the house;*

gives me a sense of instant lift-off. Why not? Why not make a willow cabin? Not, as Shakespeare had it, as a paean of love, but for retreat. A delightful bower of sappy smells and no window. And why have I let another season pass without making my tent of roses? Every year I intend to construct a flowery sanctuary for summer, a kind of octagonal marquee made from climbing roses, all whites, creams and sulphurs. It will be very closely restrained to keep its shape with no fuzziness from little sprigs and wayward buds. On midsummer noons full of shadows and fragrance I shall sit under the elegant bones of the iron structure rising like a rib-cage, while outside the roses will look like a garment of silk embroidery where the light catches the edge of each petal.

In lots of places there are people who do not just talk about garden ideas, but who actually do them. Determined and resolute, with their sketches by their side, they set out to make follies and *potagers*, frail trellises and blue pavilions, around which they plant their pinks and silvers. But my idea for a living bridge made of willows is long past its sell-by date: I no longer have a stream running through my garden, as I did when, standing by our bedroom window looking at the brook, I thought how pretty it would be to have a pair of willows, one on each bank, intertwining each other across the water. The walking bit could be made of cleft oak, and the handrails would be made from plaited willows dangling with catkins in the spring. And when we lived in Greece I contemplated a kind of trampoline or vast hammock in the olive trees just outside our bedroom window, where, on moonlit nights,

I could gently surge like a roller at sea and watch the stars between the freckled leaves. There is no doubt that gardening sparks off hare-brained ideas. But luckily we have our saner moments or how else would anyone make a garden?

On Corfu we had a courtyard, large and walled, with iron gates on three sides, a lemon tree (never without fruit even while in blossom), two mandarin trees, a Pepper Tree (*Schinus molle*), and what the locals called a Persian lilac: a sixty-foot evergreen tree with creamy flowers, never correctly identified but nothing like the eight-foot shrub called *Syringa* x *persica*. A wisteria, as writhing as a python, laid its contorted folds along the top of the wall and over a pergola; self-seeded mulleins (rejected by grazing animals) thrust their yellow tapers out of grey-green woolly rosettes with the same arbitrary casualness as asphodels which grew among the hills and scrubby land around us. Iris and roses, tree peonies and bridal wreath strayed everywhere, that is until the day summer began, when annihilation banished everything. Within a week a dusty and languid look overcame the lot as we settled in for drought for the next five months.

Only the plumbago, as cleanly blue as folds in a pure cotton sheet, remained impervious: reaching fourteen feet up the wall and spreading out on either side, the shrub never flinched for months; its brittle twigginess, light green leaves and cascade of flowers stayed unwilting throughout the summer. Myrtle, just outside the gates, also took summer in its stride. According to Oleg Polunin and Anthony Huxley in their *Flowers of the Mediterranean* when the nymph Daphne turned into myrtle to escape Apollo's ardour: 'this botanically misleading episode results in classically-minded Greeks calling the myrtle, Daphne.' Who's fussing? The evergreen myrtle, with its aromatic leaves and nondescript flowers smelling faintly of bottled fruit juice, deserves respect; like the donkey, it too once had its hour. Bound into wreaths myrtle crowned the brows of poets, magistrates and victorious competitors in the Olympic games.

In the hot months of summer, pots, which are a chore to water but which can usefully be grouped according to what is in the pink that week, kept our courtyard flowery until the day when, after the first rain, cyclamen and sternbergias – the lily-of-the-field, as brightly varnished as chrome marsh marigolds – appeared from the unprepossessing soil under the Persian lilac. For those of us brought up on drizzle, having no weeding to do for months seemed an odd way of gardening, but the burnt brown grass, flowing away under olive and cypress trees for month after month, meant manic jubilation when the first, almost hallucinatory green, appeared in October.

In 1910 Sophie Atkinson, a young Englishwoman, went to Corfu to stay with friends who lived in a house overlooking the straits towards the Greek mainland and Albania. Her descriptions of the wild flowers, olive gathering and pressing, of the markets, fishing boats and her winter excursions by bicycle or carriage into the northern villages, are vividly recounted in her book, *An Artist in Corfu*, published in 1911. She writes of the Venetian house where she stayed, with its double staircase leading up to the entrance and the huge double doors below which led into wine-making vaults: 'I think the situation of the Dousmani's house is unsurpassed by any in the island. It is surrounded to its walls with olives and flowering trees and vineyards . . .'

She describes how, when the heat was intolerable, 'the hammocks hang just beyond the courtyard wall . . . between four great olive trunks, and this summer drawing-room is roofed with a dense woven thatch of wisteria-green when the tasseled silken pavilion of spring has vanished. The long lazy afternoons are spent there, half asleep in the heat . . .'

More than half a century later, when the house belonged to us, during those stupefying weeks of summer we used to have our lunch sitting on a hunk of wood which had come out of the olive press, with our backs against the courtyard wall, and think of Sophie. We called the four olives 'Sophie's trees': the same great trees she described. Ah, Sophie, where are the originals of the watercolours in your book? And how many others, delicate and detailed, did you paint as you wandered across the island escorted by a small boy carrying your painting gear? Do they by chance still lie neglected in some forgotten folio?

Olive trees (the ones where I wanted my trampoline), grew right up to the house, just as Sophie described them, and in one a fragrant white *Rosa banksiae* curled forty feet into the branches outside our bedroom window. Near the tree were oleanders: evergreen bushes with flowers the shape of periwinkles, the colour of roses. Others were white and so silvery at dusk that when outlines had merged and the fireflies were pulsating under the trees, the flowers appeared incandescent in the breathless air which never brought relief. Their lush opulence belies their character; bark, leaf, flower and wood are deadly poisonous. If you skewered meat for grilling with a piece of oleander or inhaled the smoke from the leaves and twigs, you would live to regret it – no, that's not right – you couldn't, you'd be dead.

In many gardens in France the pots of oleanders had to be brought indoors during four months of winter, but here they were everywhere – their favourite habitats were river beds, gravelly sites or the abandoned dereliction surrounding crumbling villas long ago neglected by owners who had forsaken their properties for the more jazzy life of Athens. And if you have the opportunity to travel to Greece in early summer, take the railway from Dhiakofto, which lies on the coastal road between Corinth and Patras, to Kalavrita. Within fourteen miles you rise to 2300 feet, passing through a forbidding gorge beside a wild and boulder-strewn river where the wild oleanders almost brush the sides of the narrow rack-and-pinion train. Halfway up there is a halt for the monastery, Megaspeleion, where, years ago, there used to be the smallest, most unpretentious auberge in the world, where the table for eating outside was placed on the other side of the track. It's years since I was there, but I still remember vividly as I looked out at the rugged landscape the cloying scent of the fluffy pink and white oleander flowers drifting in through the open windows of the train.

Our first serious encounter with oleanders, though we had passed them in profusion through Attica, Thessaly and Thrace, growing out of stony ground where seemingly there was not a drop of water, was in 1953. We were travelling for three months on a journey through Yugoslavia, Greece and Turkey. In those days each traveller was allowed to take only £50 out of the country, so eating was frugal and sleeping was in a flimsy tent wherever we happened to land up each night.

The night of the oleanders was in the heart of Greece, in the Peloponnese, the country called Arcadia. In an orchard of figs, vines and wild oleanders where we needed no tent, the heat was so relentless, we slept under the stars enveloped by oleanders. Long ago Arcadia was a land of warriors and musicians, who thought themselves 'more ancient than the moon', and of shepherds who lived on acorns. Pan, the god of shepherds, lived among them, when he wasn't off deceiving nymphs. The mixture of dark local wine, with which a nearby shepherd had plied us, and the soporific and nutty scent of the oleanders, were both potent enough to make us swear that when travel was easier we'd return to Greece.

Years later we did return. And it was on Corfu, on a midsummer noon when the whole island was suspended in sleep with neither a beginning nor an end, that I sensed the ghosts. Sitting among the oleanders and Sophie's trees, half mesmerized and supine, above the screaming arc of the cicadas I could easily imagine I heard that age-old lament – an eerie cry, mournful and most dreadful, echoing across the still waters of the Ionian sea: 'The – great – god – Pan – is – dead.'

And it was on this part of our land, before the drought had overcome us and before the oleanders were in flower, that each year the ground was covered with white flowers: the closely-growing stars of Bethlehem and small white alliums which, much later in my life, goaded me into trying to grow others of the family in our garden in England.

Onions that flower in summer have impeccable symmetry. They are not to be despised, these alliums smelling of the chopping board; their spherical heads of blues and cloudy pinks, their strappy leaves, fit into the garden like coloured lollipops rising above the panniered skirts of roses as agreeably as verbascums or foxgloves.

The range of alliums is varied, choice is perplexing. *Allium caeruleum* is small with densely packed blue flowers which can form a frilly hem to some sumptuous yellow rose. Tall alliums like *A. christophii* look incomparable thrusting their spiky orbs of filigree mauve through silvery pink blooms of 'Madame Pierre Oger' or rising above the languishing grace of the 'Duchesse de Montebello', pink and drowsing in her own fragrance. *A. karataviense* is an imposing bulb only about eight inches high but with greyish-pink flowers more than six inches across appearing as if made from finely-wrought metal.

Greedily, one summer, I tried to grow a six-foot allium, *A. giganteum*. I imagined these puce monsters levitating above the roses like floating spheres of some unearthly form of thistledown. It didn't work. Their colour is hideous – like the blossom of Judas trees – and the ungainly stems were disproportionately stout for the circumference of the heads. But I shall not be put off. The *Liliaceae/Alliaceae* family is versatile: there are spring-flowering alliums and dwarf rosy ones; delicate pink puffs, clumpy yellow bells or domed magenta globules. *A. albopilosum*, a native of Persia, may not be a name which has instant appeal but its quivering globe of deep lilac looks airborne when in flower, and in winter turns to the warm colour of chaff. It is a virtuoso at dying, as is the rest of the tribe, making any flower-arranger avid to add them to their collection of artichoke heads.

Alliums and roses go together as compatibly as buddlejas with railway lines. The sight of buddlejas clinging onto life among the bricks and detritus outside Euston or Paddington station is a proof of stamina and an uplift to the heart. What tenacity. What will-power for life. The shrubs are nurtured on fumes and sullied rain; how perverse and curious. Are they telling us something? Has a railway environment the elixir of life for buddlejas? Every gardener has at one time or another attempted to grow plants which go against the grain of the garden's own persona. No one goes to Alsace to drink Bordeaux wine or to the Périgord to eat *choucroute*. So why do some gardeners feel challenged to grow sweet peas in the tropics or a lawn in New South Wales, or make a Japanese garden in the Scottish Borders? No amount of coercion would persuade a magnolia to grow for us in the rugged hills of Shropshire, however fawningly we cosseted each replaced victim. In the end we accepted the buddleja's message. Plants communicate their preferences; the buddleja's are explicit, so were our magnolias', their pathetic cries for help almost audible as they succumbed to frost.

There is said to be a symbiosis between owners and their pets. People who keep a dog or a goat are supposed to grow to look like them: a kind of physical coalescence surreptitiously develops between human and beast, which slowly becomes recognizable in the way they whimper or lift their upper lips. That may be so. But gardens certainly do reflect their owners. Some gardens appear as trim as ironed hankies while others are as romantic as Brahms. And though these places, whatever their style, are as ephemeral as *Rosa sancta* in June, while each owner has

his or her own hand on the trowel the garden's personality is integral. Their fingerprints are everywhere. Walk into a garden, and before you meet the owner, you can have a fairly strong inkling of what sort of person will appear. Not necessarily the outward form, but if he or she is truly the person who does the actual gardening, the inner, rather than the everyday mind, is revealed by their garden.

But there are other gardens: the impersonal, the public or the municipal private gardens. In London where I grew up, on summer mornings when the sky was a cloudless washed-out blue, hazy from pollution, there was a low hum of traffic; a low purr that was only audible on still days of summer. And I hated it. London was bearable in rain, when the buses were lit up inside throughout the day, but in fine weather I pined for the country and used to dread with misgiving dawns of filmy skies. Anyone who has had to make do with the shabby grass of a London park and pretend they were in pastoral heaven knows how sterile that self-fooling can be. It broke my heart. I could not accept the way things were; I regarded every regimented tulip as an outrageous travesty.

And yet, and yet – London squares! The intervening years have changed my focus. They are places of such secrecy I still seek them out. Railed around and private with their gates kept locked, when glimpsed from the top of a bus each appears as a green oasis. Plane trees held as though underwater stand motionless and gloomy among flowerless beds of shrubs. Shrubs so self-effacing they are impossible to identify. Bloomsbury, Belgravia, Kensington or Notting Hill Gate, wherever the gardens are, they hark back to security and comfort, to orderliness and exclusion. Developed in the nineteenth century many of these gardens were concealed by the houses backed around them so securely that not a breath of exhaust nor the grinding of gears ever penetrates their privacy. Do other capitals have such retreats dotted about the city like viridian splodges on the surface of a toad?

Far removed from the intimate design of London squares is Central
Park in New York, a huge piece of landscaped land used by every sort of
person looking for space in the midst of concrete. And at its north end,
about where 104th Street joins Fifth Avenue, is a delightful six-acre
garden overlooked by the tall buildings of apartments, museums and a
hospital.

The reasons for it being called the Conservatory Garden have long
since disappeared: the glasshouses were dismantled in 1934 and the
garden successfully maintained until around the late 1960s when the
usual malaise crept in – shortage of money. Dereliction, embellished by
graffiti, slowly eroded the garden until it no longer drew visitors from all
over the city to enjoy its floral charm. Miraculously, by the end of the
1970s, people who cared passionately and had been saddened by the
garden's decline decided to do something about it. They were
volunteers from the Garden Club of America. With zeal and enthusiasm

they planted bright annuals, restored the fountains and with hearty determination breathed life back into the garden. By 1982, with a very generous grant from the Rockefeller Center to Central Park Conservancy, the restoration work really took off.

Lynden Miller, the imaginative and energetic director of the Conservatory Garden, spoke of its restoration as we walked along the paths where young gardeners were busy on their knees preparing for spring.

The garden is divided into three areas: the north part has a fountain and concentric beds of seasonal flowers from bulbs to chrysanthemums, and four arches covered by 'Silver Moon' rambler roses with glossy leaves and clusters of buttery buds which open in June into creamy-white flowers smelling of apples. In the central garden are lawns flanked by yew hedges and magnificent crab apple *allées* which, when we were there in March, formed an avenue of intricate black tracery from their contorted limbs. And at the end of the lawns, backing a water jet in the centre of a pool, are tiered hedges rising to a very fine iron pergola entwined by the sinuous coils of a fifty-year-old wisteria.

The south garden, which had been in the saddest state, was resuscitated entirely thanks to the generosity of supporters living in the neighbourhood. The beds have now been planted with perennials; the small pool, with a bronze statue in memory of the author of *The Secret Garden* – Frances Hodgson Burnett – has been repaired; and in May, Mrs Miller told us, the place is redolent with the scent of the hundreds of lilac trees that surround the garden. Beyond, on the woodland slopes, are ferns and wild flowers. Enough money was raised to pay for a full-time gardener, supported by a seemingly unending supply of urban volunteers devoted to cherishing their city garden.

The day we were there the weather was freaky: it was 86°F. The trees were leafless, flowers fugitive, but people were drawn to the garden like bees to a lime tree. With sleeves rolled up they ate their lunchtime sandwiches, lolled on seats or strolled along the paths. We were told by Mrs Miller that all through the year school parties, disabled groups, bird watchers and picknickers continually visit and revisit the gardens, regardless of the weather: a momentary escape from the concrete jungle.

City gardens form the linchpin to a metropolis – whether in New York, Paris, Tokyo or Sydney. They provide urban sanctuaries to restore our lungs and our spirits from insalubrity. But what of future summers? We already have irradiated food so how much longer before we are faced with irradiated gardens? Imagine garden centres selling dead-straight plants guaranteed against wilt and blackspot; immune from thrips. Think of the clove-scented pink and candelabra primula, the pasque flower and comely acanthus all exposed to the stainless-steel rods of cobalt-60. Irradiation is poetically described as an enriched incarnation of the naturally occurring cobalt-59; a radioactive isotope emitting gamma rays with as much abandon as a tobacco plant at dusk emits scent. But do we want such plants? Do we need flowers to last the summer? Think of it. One outing to a plant nursery and the whole garden could be kitted out.

Eventually a garden could last a lifetime, with gamma rays spreading like hairspray over imperishable euphorbias and solanums. It would be the end of unpredictability. With a dose of kilogray (kGy, I am told, is the unit of measurement for the absorbed dose of gamma radiation) away would go stupefaction. But the fallibility of flowers is their charm; lamenting, gloating or guilt are part of the enigma of gardening. Stainless-steel encased pencils of cobalt-60, their enriched incarnations, their isotopes emitting gamma rays, may read like poetry, but it is a bit of verse we can do without.

Meanwhile, this summer, I want to forget forebodings about methane gas emissions transmitting their way thermodynamically into the ozone layer; I do not want to brood on tropospheric ozone, chlorofluorocarbons, nitrous oxide and carbon dioxide getting at our climate. The thought that one day Morning Glories may festoon the granite of Aberdeen leaves me cold. Instead I shall shorten my sights and focus on a mallow or a poppy, whose flowers look more like scraps of crumpled silk than petals on the point of opening. We may, as human beings, be 'thinking reeds' but at this precise moment I want to give up on bleak prophesies, think about giraffes, and smell a rose not an allium.

CHAPTER VI
A WILDLY UNSYMMETRICAL MESS
Conjecture

PECIALISTS WHO SPEND THEIR TIME DISCUSSING THE correct nomenclature of a particular dianthus rather than seeing the overall cohesion of a garden underline the existence of two types of gardener. There are Plants People; avid collectors who rise to a challenge; who safeguard rarities, and to whom future generations will be indebted for saving from extinction some precious plant on the brink of vanishing through negligence. This fervour can be carried a bit far. At the extreme of bigotry, a snowdrop pundit dismisses my job lot of white flummery spreading under the trees in February: 'Dig them up! Get different specimen snowdrops. Plant them in family groups.' And as a final broadside: 'And be sure to label them!'

The other sort are us. People who garden. People who buy on impulse and plant intuitively, and who bumble about learning as they go. People who often in the end and quite by chance create such places of beauty that every year devotees will eagerly scan the latest Yellow Book (the annual *Gardens of England & Wales Open to the Public*, published by the National Gardens Scheme) to find out when their gardens will be open.

I have come to the conclusion that those who visit gardens only metamorphose into human beings when the new Yellow Book appears in the bookshops each spring. It took me some years of having our

93

garden open before I realized that once this species of enthusiast has left the garden threshold they vanish off the face of the earth. Where to? Where does it go, this enchanting breed of *Homo sapiens*? These aficionados who quietly stroll, who are appreciative and so tidy? I have never met them anywhere else. Not on station platforms, not in market squares, not round historical sites or at self-service restaurants. Only a 'Garden Open' brings them forth: sweet and gentle people, who say thank you for opening your garden and how lovely it has been and how pretty are the roses and I never thought of gardening like this. Communicative and smiling, they moon among the flowers as though they had descended that afternoon from some celestial Elysium. And after they have gone nothing unwelcome remains – no paper, no debris, no trace that they were real – except for a small residue of niceness which, like pollen, has rubbed off on us so that, however exhausting the preparation for this event has been, we vow to each other that next year we must do it again. (There are gardeners who say they do lose cuttings from opening their gates to the public, but with us this never happened for the simple reason there was nothing worth taking. Our plants were commoners.)

Of course I know what it is, this benign manifestation which invaded our garden: alchemy. The invisible element which mysteriously hangs around garden paths with as much potency as when base metal turns to gold. Where else, tell me, can you find such felicity in a place as ubiquitous as a garden?

But what is it with men? Given half a chance they would condemn trees for having leaves. They would banish them from the garden for their unruly habits; for producing crispy debris that needs clearing up. If only these garden custodians would stop; use other eyes, and see that conventional responses imbibed from childhood could be stood on their head and that leaves in autumn left lying on the ground create an encircling amber or topaz pool the dimension of the branches.

Whatever gets into men once they are gardening? They become obsessed with tidiness. I bet they aren't like that in the bedroom.

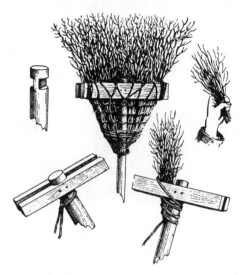

A friend wrings his hands over the nature of dog violets: their habit of propagating themselves untidily about his paths sends him wild with rage. Geoffrey Grigson, in *The Englishman's Flora*, lists fifty-seven plants called 'dog'. But why? (Not why does he list them, but why 'dog'?) It seems to be a pejorative tag, often used to distinguish the less classy form of wild flower, such as the dog rose from the garden one; or dog's mercury, a useless relative of annual mercury which was used in medicine; or dogwood, whose berries aren't fit to be eaten by human *or* dog.

Another gardener, who has a fine and large town garden, admits that he banished buddlejas for their disorderly habits. Yet another cannot stand the sight of ivy-leafed toadflax scrambling between the bricks of his lovely old walls and 'messing up' his clematis. Until every strand is

pulled out he cannot feel at peace; he begins at one end of the garden and with ruthless single-mindedness tweaks away every scrap of this lilac-flowered creeper, but to his anguish the plant has a crafty tendency to turn its seed-heads away from the light, thereby securing its immortality by filling the mortar with next year's crop. Even Harold Nicolson found his wife's ardour for romantic dishevelment went against the grain in the garden at Sissinghurst.

Vita Sackville-West. Her words echo down the years; her influence is still blossoming in countless gardens today. She once wrote: 'For my own part, if I were suddenly required to leave my own garden and to move into a bungalow on a housing estate, or into a council house, I should have no hesitation at all about ruffling the front garden into a wildly unsymmetrical mess . . .' We, having known Miss Sackville-West through reading her articles and books and from walking the paths of Sissinghurst, now have an intoxicating vision of this distinguished gardener turning a small garden of something like ten yards by twenty into a ravishing cornucopia of reckless colour and confusion. 'A wildly unsymmetrical mess.' How corruptive! What divisive inspiration her words engender. And how far that leads us away from the copybook conformity dished out ad nauseam in the popular press and over the air.

If Vita Sackville-West were alive today surely she would be on the side of the luminaries: those garden writers who do inspire us to question and rebel, those who remind us that wild flowers are in retreat, under threat; a situation which will, in the end, compromise the whole wildlife cycle. The plaint is appalling, and though we hear of it year after year until we can no longer grasp its enormity, the facts are brutal.

In these islands almost half our ancient woodland has been destroyed; ninety-seven per cent of wildflower meadows and more than half our peat bogs have vanished, as well as so many miles of hedgerow they could encircle the earth seven times over. According to the *British Red Data Book for Vascular Plants* (which details all Britain's Extinct, Endangered, Vulnerable and Rare plants), two thirds of the localities known to contain rare wild flowers have already vanished. Because flowers are found in the wild, are these plants to be verbally jettisoned as weeds?

Rather, our derogatory attitude should be turned inside out; no one surely, with eyes to see, would condemn wood-sorrel, campion, stitchwort or speedwell because they go walkabout along banks, among crops or sidle through our lawns? Only the visually prejudiced could fail to see the beauty of hart's-tongue fern or dog's mercury, or the nobility of butterburrs, even though some of these plants can become a little pushy in parts of the garden. It is imperative to safeguard what we have not only from the plough, drainage, herbicides and development, but from gardeners dead set on rounding up any pretty flower they find for free.

I can imagine Vita Sackville-West eloquently pleading with us to keep a corner of the garden for wilderness. But what flowers would she

revere? What floral 'weeds' would she suggest we encourage to seed and flourish in our gardens? The choice is immense yet we need to be selective, and without her eloquence, her imagination and pungent prose to guide us we must fend for ourselves when it comes to alternatives.

One of my favourite plants is the celandine. If I were to choose five wild flowers (apart from the obvious primrose, cowslip and bluebell), I think I would go for the lesser celandine, *Ranunculus ficaria*, belonging to the same family as the buttercup but having such a different posture. I love their glossy flowers and heart-shaped leaves which hug the ground and seem almost to sprinkle shady places in early spring between one sunset and the following sunrise. By August they have vanished; not a trace remains to show they were ever here. Celandines have nothing like the grace of windflowers, the robust stance of the field scabious, nor the clandestine behaviour of the dog violet but, small and crouching as they are, they throw out a kind of glittering vitality which comes from the way the plants look perfectly crafted and very chipper. Wordsworth, who was so enamoured of them that they are carved on his tomb, wrote these unbelievably downbeat lines:

> *There's a flower that shall be mine,*
> *'Tis the little celandine.*

Lady's Smock is a flower I want to stray into the garden. Commonly called Cuckoo Flower because it arrives with the bird, and often known as Milkmaids, *Cardamine pratensis* is an independent plant which refuses to be herded. The flowers are nothing: four little petals on each floret which are rather haphazardly arranged at the end of a slender stem. They appear to have been made from fabric so often washed its pallid lilac has almost been rinsed away. But their charm lies in the way they sway in the slightest breeze and their undemonstrative form adds a milky-mauve brush stroke as a foil to more masterful flowers. Perhaps their Somerset local name, Naked Ladies, does have some hallucinatory logic.

Would Vita Sackville-West harbour willowherb, *Epilobium montanum*, I wonder? A plant which frequents gardens in spring with its shiny leaves and maddening good health whatever the winter has been like. Lovely as the flower is, its downy seeds spread so abundantly that even the most ardent supporter may rue the day they allowed it to proliferate. But it is a beauty. Another of the willowherb family, *Chamerion angustifolium*, poetically known as Rose Bay and more than four feet tall, has spires of rosy-purple flowers loved by bees, and narrow leaves not unlike the willow. It arrives as if by some wily stratagem onto city building sites. The bombed wreckage of London wasteland became outlandishly transformed by an expanse of pinkness among the debris. In America too, where the plant takes over land that has recently been burnt, the flower is known not only as Fireweed but also Bay Willow or Purple Rocket. And around Seattle, according to Geoffrey Grigson,

Fireweed honey is produced by bees passionate for the nectar in spite of getting liberally smeared with sticky pollen.

But one wild flower I long to tempt into my garden is the bright pink musk mallow, *Malva moschata*, whose leaves in warm weather do smell a bit musky. It belongs to a vast family of around a thousand species that includes such imposing plants as hollyhocks and the hibiscus, which requires a bit of petting to grow successfully in England. Once I saw these mallows, as pink as the flowers of *Rosa californica plena*, trickling along the edge of a densely planted field of flax in East Anglia. The blue of the crop was neither of the sea nor of the sky, it was too intense, too opaque. Reaching unbroken to the horizon, with the border of mallow frilling the field, the sight was implausible. In a painting it would have looked like the aberration of an over-saccharined imagination.

Because I am now making a garden in a town I am excluded from the prodigious number of wild flowers that used to inhabit our country garden. Here I have a long, narrow plot where in spring there were small clutches of willowherb and one or two thrusting floxglove leaves as well as ivy-leafed toadflax looking so much like a network of feather stitch I wanted it everywhere.

At the far end, in the corner of the garden, is an elder, a tree of the countryside rather than urban back gardens, but commonly spread by starlings gorging on the berries. Half tree, half bush, growing in a crouched position with fissured bark, it smells both sweet and repulsive. Not until the flowers appear is summer said to have arrived. Flat-topped and fragrant, the flowers form a luxuriant creamy profusion which when they die leave dismal green foliage reminiscent of the municipal paint used so unimaginatively on park benches. But in autumn comes a reward: the berries. Glossy as funeral jewellery, immune to pollution, tasting sweet yet bland when eaten raw, the berries were used for generations to make an almost black wine. Even so the tree gets a bad press.

Christ was nailed to a cross made of elder, Judas hanged himself from it (difficult, you would think, considering the size of the tree), and just listen to this from *The Englishman's Flora*: 'In the Middle Ages, Jacobus

de Voragine says that before the Passion the Elder was a tree of shame, used for the execution of criminals; a tree of darkness, being dark and without beauty; a tree of death, since men were put to death upon it; and a tree of evil smell, because it was planted in the midst of rotting corpses.' A description hardly likely to get the elder into an arboreal Honours List.

But if that's not enough to condemn it forever to damnation, the litany of malediction goes on: associated with the devil for centuries, the 'stinking' Elder must neither be brought into the house nor must it be burnt. (Even today some woodmen refuse to cut down the 'Ellan wood', as it is still called in parts of Gloucestershire.) And, according to Linnaeus, goats, who are by no means picky eaters, will not touch the elder. On May Day the leaves were used as protection from witches; when bruised the leaves had such a repulsive smell they were worn in hats to keep midges away; the bark was used in black dye, and elderflower water was used by our great-great-grandmothers for their complexions and as tea for 'inducing free perspiration'. The uses of bark, root, leaf and flower are legion. Disdained and forsaken as the tree is, the Boon Tree, as it was sometimes called, has a pedigree reaching far back into the realms of ritual practice and sympathetic magic.

Creeping under the branches of the elder, smelling again that familiar metallic scent, I go to pull out unwanted nettles and general town detritus which seems always to surface from nowhere: fragments of intricately patterned crockery, shattered slivers of green glass worn smooth at the edges, rusty hinges surviving long after the worm-eaten door has decayed, and vacated snail shells surviving their decomposed occupants are proof that traditionally the tree was planted beside rubbish heaps. When we were children the elder in the garden of a flint and brick house in Buckinghamshire provided a perfect place for my sister and me to hide. Apart from a sharp twinge and momentary annoyance from the brittle twigs catching at our hair, the circle around the buckled trunk offered us the perfect sanctuary for hide-and-seek and eluding adults.

So this elder, in the far corner of my garden, takes up space I could well use for something sophisticated and dashing. But how can I move 'God's Stinking Tree'? With such a history; with its superstitions, legends, folklore; its use in medicine from the ague to the plague; its use

as cordials and for jazzing up British port; its significance to writers such as Pliny, Shakespeare, Spenser, John Evelyn, and even William Langland in his allegorical poem *Piers Plowman*, my *Sambucus nigra* remains secure. Safe, the fairly lacklustre tree, weedy in appearance with its weight of symbolism and prejudice, provides me with a secret refuge when the Furies are closing in.

I have also inherited a ruffian. An army of ruffians. Bindweed: with the prettiest flower and an indomitable life force. A ceaseless pogrom must be carried out against this louche trespasser and even then, before I start, I know I am defeated. If only its disposition were chivalrous, not murderous, convolvulus would be angelic to have twining like a clematis with grace among the roses. But not so. It may have decorative flowers in late summer, but what a mobster. Without any sense of proportion it gets everywhere: dead set on throttling roses, peonies, buddlejas or cistus. I am doomed, according to gardening friends, to live with it. 'A fiend! An utter fiend!' And they shrug eloquently that there is nothing to be done; if you fail to dig it up completely and a root breaks off (which it invariably does), that encourages further fulsome growth.

This scourge runs from garden to garden, leaping walls, insinuating itself through hedges, and tunnelling underground with unreasonable tenacity. I try to feel differently towards it, to feel tolerant, philosophical and to have a certain detached benevolence. And if it were not so set on strangulation I would succeed; I could change my attitude of mind and come to love it. In Greece we did. But there the convolvulus tribe knew its place and every year a lovely blue twiner twisted its way up the iron banisters of the double flight of stone steps leading to the front door, never rampaging but always remaining obligingly decorous.

Now I am growing another of the family; a stranger. It is the first time I have had this unbelievable beauty within my grasp. *Convolvulus cneorum*. I can't believe it: it's been in flower off and on for months. It is a thing of such exquisite loveliness I don't understand why *C. mauritanicus* is always given a higher profile – it's a dream, of course, with its trails of blue flowers groping across the ground – but this one of mine, which is mentioned only once, unlike the blue one, in the half dozen books I've just looked through, has grown into a low mound of silvery weightlessness from silky leaves radiating light. The flowers, springing out from stout clusters, are white; fragile as butterfly wings with five faded-pink spokes radiating from a yellow eye. A vase of them stands beside me as I write. I know that by early evening every petal will be furled as each flower closes down for the night. In the morning they wait until I draw back the curtains before opening. Then, while I have them in the house, I am torn with indecision: do the flowers or the cat take precedence? Both are importunate in their different ways.

I have to add a rider to my condemnation of bindweed. As I thought, I never was in control of the thug, so I am not surprised to find that by October bits I had overlooked have grown so immense they reach far into the forty-foot holly which grows at the end of my garden beside the elder. And it looks wonderful. The white flowers are in full spate among the shiny leaves and bright red berries of the holly.

A lot of gardening could be up-ended. Things which cause outrage can be looked at from a different angle and we can recover equipoise. Take dandelions. My neighbour's wide lawn is strewn with them in May and he despairs. What is he to do? If it were not for his pets he would spray the whole area with weedkiller, rotavate and re-sow grass seed, he says. But look at these weeds dispassionately: if you did not know they were classified as weeds and so common at that, dandelions would be commendable. Speckled yellow among the green – how decorative. Probably in other parts of the world, where dandelions are not indigenous, they would be considered most recherché. But my neighbour does not see it like that. To him they are pariahs. As soon as he has mown, up they spring to dot the green with yellow blobs with such vigorous audacity my neighbour feels humiliated. A contrary slant on the flowers and he could rejoice at the same time as lowering his blood pressure.

My garden has no lawn because last winter I took it all up. After one summer of fiddling about with the mower, of attempting to be dextrous when lowering or raising the blades and keeping them unclogged from wads of damp grass while not being electrocuted, I decided it was absurd. Life should be simpler than this. The results didn't even look good when I'd mown; for one thing I never swept up the cuttings; for another the grass around shrubs remained tangled; and in other parts I had somehow left the lawn with patches of brown flesh exposed. What a futile weekly chore when other sorts of gardening offer such spiritual regeneration.

We are supposed to have lawns in England; that is our thing. But years ago, before I moved into a town, I read David Hicks's terse advice in *Garden Design* that for anyone with a small garden it was a waste of time growing a lawn. After that first summer I took his advice; in place of grass I have laid four inches of bark spread across the ground like grated chocolate. What effect it will have on the shrubs growing out of the bark, I have not yet had time to discover, but I get a certain contemplative serenity gazing at the stuff from an upstairs window as background to small eucalyptus trees the colour of the Atlantic in winter.

Having not one meaningful tree in the garden except for an elder and a holly, in the last six months I have planted twenty-seven trees. Huge ones – if I let them have their heads. But I will not. Eight are limes, *Tilia platyphyllos* 'Rubra', planted along the fence, which I shall pleach. Already I have decapitated them at twelve feet high, tying their slender twiggy side branches down to canes which run horizontally from tree to tree so that eventually they will look like a row of dancers holding hands. Others are twelve eucalyptus, the kind commonly grown in Britain for being one of the hardiest, *Eucalyptus gunnii*. I am experimenting: wanting to see if I can cut them into rather openwork airy spheres, the greyish-green of corroded copper, flanking the straight cobbled path from the house to the far end of the garden where I have put a door going nowhere. Everything diminishes: the path very slightly tapers to give the illusion of distance, and leads to a short flight of narrowing steps where the door, only five feet high, is framed by two scaled-down wooden arches. Around the arches I have planted honeysuckle and

roses to give a tunnel effect which I hope will eventually look shadowy and tempting.

Flowers are a blight in gardens. No, of course I don't mean that. But they can be overdone – like wearing too much jewellery, or a plate of *nouvelle cuisine* over-garnished with kiwi fruit and a pool of rubescent *coulis*. Certain French gardeners I met had an enviable discriminatory eye where their flowers were concerned. Their austere garden designs were imaginatively but very selectively touched up with flowers.

In this garden, so different from our previous wild one, I am dead set on mutilation. Preserved like flies in amber, my memories of French gardens have trapped me. My shrubs and trees are doomed. Amputation will be inflicted on everything wilful or ebullient, except for a few extroverts – certain roses – which I shall allow to behave wantonly. But two weeping willows, the commonplace *Salix purpurea* 'Pendula', have already had their tresses shorn so that now they stand with bobbed heads, circular and leafy, at two corners of a small paved sitting area I intend to make secretive and enclosed.

Two rounded balls of box mark the entrance, and more box, interspersed with larger shrubs, surrounds the 'terrace', the size of a tablecloth. I hope, one day, the box hedging will make geometric lines stringing one shrub to another like beads on a thread. An Irish yew, which I'll keep as narrow as a cat's tail – the nearest I can get to reproducing the bold black stroke of an Italian cypress – has already been cropped. As yet very small, the yew stands in the middleground. I like the effect of having an emphatic vertical beyond which, to either side and distantly, my eye is drawn to other things; half-glimpsed, they compel me to take a closer look.

My youngest daughter, Sureen, knowing my love for quince trees which grow wild in Greece and have pink blossom as brittle as porcelain before the leaves appear among the wiry rigging, unknown to me arranged for a plant nursery to deliver a quince here last Christmas Eve. What a present. I would never had had the imagination to plant one of those in my town garden. Bare-rooted, it went in hurriedly on Christmas Day without much forethought about the placement. Later in the year the tree was covered with blossom, and though I don't hold out much hope of any fruit maturing, the sight of so many flowers in its first spring gives me confidence to think that we did plant it in the right place.

Other trees have gone in with a sense of urgency: I want to be able to walk not 'in' my garden but 'through' it. This feeling only works for me once I am overshadowed by trees or by garlanded structures taller than myself. At present everything here is skeletal – horizontal and visible at one glance – but I need to walk among things; to weave, move round, sidestep, bend and dodge; to brush against and disentangle; to shrug off predatory tendrils and duck under illusionary boughs. Alpines, annuals, parterres, knot gardens and rockeries are fine for those who want them, but unless there are places to stoop and sidle I have no sense of 'being' in the garden. Of being there, and of feeling wholly and unreservedly integrated into its completeness.

There is a time for staying still, and a time for moving on. Events have changed what I wanted to remain static, yet now they have happened unforeseen alternatives appeared. Alternatives with their own impetus, unpremeditated and peremptory. What I am making in my garden now is far from where my instinct led me ten years ago.

CHAPTER VII

A THREE-DIMENSIONAL EYE
Looking

G OD WILL NOT LET ME BELIEVE IN HIM, WHICH MEANS that when things go right I have no one to thank. Nor to canvass when things go wrong. My sister died at thirty-eight years old and at the time, though I was four years younger, I thought I had more strength than her to die. I don't know what gave me such self-confidence except that, in my youth, I'd been half in love with easeful death – calling him soft names since adolescence. But she, my older sister – protector and comforter through childhood – had been so engrossed with her four children she had not had a moment to think about alternatives. I know differently now. Surrounded, as we are, by an obscene and vicious scourge which is not the fault of war, the young are dying. Aids scoops them up all over the world. When I grew up we had the certainty that, if we survived the bombing, old age was a probable conclusion, so we could afford our egocentric fantasies, romantic and self-indulgent, about ceasing on the midnight with no pain.

Alas, the confidence I had in my thirties has long ago deserted me, and as we cannot go home again, I look back to that time in childhood as a world of make-believe where fairy tales and confidence are irretrievably tangled in my memory as belonging to 'Once upon a time' – a kind of golden age before present worldly cynicism grew alongside children's molars. An age when, for a child, running to the letterbox was not an imprudent risk and being put on a train, into the care of a kindly stranger, was commonplace. But searching for myths is a non-starter.

I used to think dreams were the reality; if only we knew how to hold onto them – dreams were where we were at. The rest, the physical embroilment which overcame us when awake, was a fallacy. What was in my head was real – the rest was illusion. This had started when, as a child, I'd had a tooth removed by gas: for years afterwards I wondered, how could I be certain I had come round yet? There are times when I probably ought to ask myself that question again.

Imagination is a boon and a plague. You either recoil from fantasy in

fiction or become a passionate addict. R. H. Hudson's *Green Mansions*, or *One Hundred Years of Solitude* by the Colombian author Gabriel García Márquez, or *Lady Into Fox*, David Garnett's most tender story of his wife turning into a fox, being cherished by him until slowly she shows her teeth and vanishes into the wild, are stories of such spell-binding reveries they never lose their power to enthral. Without imagination we would neither have compassion nor inspiration – but it can blot out peace of mind. Cursed with it, we have been vulnerable since we went beyond mere dreaming.

Dr Anthony Storr, the psychiatrist, writes in his book *Solitude*: 'Imagination has given man flexibility; but in doing so, has robbed him of contentment.' And thus people have been dying for a myth one way or another since time began. A friend in Thailand tells the allegorical story of two monks who, upon reaching a ford, found a woman afraid to cross the water. In spite of the taboo against monks touching women, one monk picked her up and carried her to the other side, put her down and walked on. After some miles he became aware of his outraged companion. Turning to the offended monk he said: 'That girl? I put her down at the ford. Are you still carrying her?'

The answer is yes. Burdened with armfuls of dross we stagger along under the weight of accumulated guilt. Or bedevilled by remorse and frustration, fear and images, it is impossible not to be encumbered by totally useless regrets. My less ponderous ones were regrets for parts of the world I had not seen. The thought of time rushing by worked at my unease like waves against stone and I felt a restless malaise for distant journeys based on nothing more than the name of a place. Names in an atlas are such unsettlers; they cling like burrs with maddening tenacity, projecting their sense of remoteness and escape. The Karakorums; Gilgit and wild apricots; the Gobi desert with its frozen graveyard of woolly mammoths (whose stomachs were full of wild thyme, upright crowfoot and Alpine poppies); and most graphic, dreadful and illusory, a place never to be reached but only sought, a region known as the Empty Quarter.

And though some of these places are now on the tourist trail and have lost their haunting edge, I have not grown immune. A longing for remote places still chafes – such as for the Amazon in flood. I know I shall never go there, but a documentary film on the river, when great tracts of jungle were submerged, was most unsettling. The sight of drowned trees, swaying like seaweed under the river, appeared outlandish. Even the most world-weary traveller would be confounded by the appearance of fish, turtles and dolphins swimming among the tree canopy. Dolphins? It was the stuff of dreams. Certainly strong enough to unhinge complacency.

Yet I have given up fretting for the unattainable. I know I'll never watch from Parnassus the rising sun lighting up the distant Morea, nor shall I ever again float in a rice barge through the flooded paddy fields of Siam when I wanted the journey to last forever. I no longer hanker to witness a desert miracle when, after years without rain, the land bursts into flower from the first downpour. Does it really happen? I have never met anyone, not even a desert buff, who has actually been there to authenticate such an evocative legend.

However, sometimes, things do work. Once we did see migrating whales as they dived and spouted their way southwards down the coast of California. The sight of those leviathans slowly rolling through the wintry seas was well worth standing on a precipitous shore to see in a fiercely cold wind hurling itself towards us from Oregon.

Slowly, inevitably and obviously, wisely, I have knuckled under: the agitation I had for places I shall never see has lost its momentum. A comfortable acceptance has evolved, and now the scrutiny of a species tulip, with its drooping head and filigree tracings, has more consequence than far-flung places based on the flimsy provocation of a name. The fact that the flower is now the nearest I shall ever get to the High Pamirs – whose very name once made me reach for an atlas – has not actually dulled the longing, but the dynamism it once had has become mellow, less frenetic.

There are times for doing, and times for stagnating: times when, however much you want it, the moment is not now. Wishing to be where you are not is futile, but that fact has taken me years to learn.

Relinquishing a garden and settling elsewhere belongs to now – a phase out of my control. Things happen, volition shifts, and I have moved into another area. The nowness of the moment, when neither past nor future impinge, has a determination of its own so powerful at times it becomes overwhelming. Then a useful subterfuge is to sit in the garden looking at a flower through a magnifying glass, where what is revealed is of such intricacy, for those few moments, everything else falls away.

A more powerful mantra is the thought of the skeleton of a woman.

Buried two-and-a-half thousand years BC, in one of the 'Royal' tombs of the Early Dynastic Period, she was discovered by Sir Leonard Woolley. In his book *Ur of the Chaldees*, he describes the excavations. Among the ritually killed court ladies in the royal tomb of Queen Puabi, he detected a purplish stain on the skulls. These curious discolorations had been left there by the silver hair ribbons the women had worn before being murdered. But that is not all. There was one who had no such mark. Although like the others, she was wearing the great gold earrings, curled within the folds of her dress Leonard Woolley discovered a silver ribbon still unwound. The blood runs cold to read his words: 'then, as the body was cleared, there was found against it, about on the level of the waist, a flat disc a little more than 3 inches across of a grey substance which was certainly silver . . . it was a silver hair-ribbon, but it had never been worn – carried apparently in the woman's pocket, it was just as she had taken it from her room, done up in a tight coil with the ends brought over to prevent its coming undone . . .' The ends brought over to prevent it coming undone. Imagination leaps; the centuries shrivel as we wonder what had momentarily distracted her as she prepared herself for the lethal ritual. Mislaying her earrings? Her mother's tears? Her own frailty and trembling fingers? We shall never know nor can our imaginations ever lie still. Here the ribbon had lain, unknown, unremarked, for thousands of years until one day an archaeologist unearthed this piece of trivial history. The minutiae of such a detail has stayed with me for more than thirty years.

In ancient times life seemed simple; all you needed to cure a headache and to ease melancholia was a potion of violets. In medieval gardens they were grown for potpourri, for perfume, and medicinally for a multitude of ailments. Long before litmus paper, chemists used a blue syrup made from violets to identify acids and alkalis, for its facility to turn either red or green. The Doctrine of Signatures, an old and significant, if at times somewhat fanciful philosophy of medicine, tended to liken the appearance of a plant to that of a disease. For instance, the lesser celandine, whose little tubers were thought to resemble piles, was made into ointment in the belief it would cure the complaint. The root of the meadow saffron, likened to a gouty foot, was used as the panacea for this deforming disability; the leaves of pulmonarias, thought to look like lungs, were regularly used by apothecaries for diseases of that organ. Because Parsley Breakstone, smaller than the common Lady's Mantle and known as Parsley Piert or Bowel-hive-grass, grows in dry soil and on

the tops of walls, it was believed to break up stones in the bladder or kidneys. Some remedies worked more than others. Eyebright, with its open bloodshot flowers has, for generations, been a classic cure for eye afflictions and no doubt the sweet violet, with its heart-shaped leaves, is the reason why it was thought 'to comfort and strengthen the heart'.

' "I never saw anybody that looked stupider," a Violet said, so suddenly, that Alice quite jumped . . .'. In *Through the Looking Glass* Lewis Carroll attributes to this flower a far more caustic tongue than I would have expected after looking closely at their faces.

Now, and I don't know how it's happened, violas and pansies have appeared like a deep indigo dye soaking through the pages of this book. Ought I to apologize because here they come again? Perhaps it's because the flowers are universally available with their familiar demeanour, and maybe too because they are found in natural habitats as diverse as the blandly pastoral and the raw wilderness.

They are flowers to which there has to be some sort of response, however dedicated to the smell of diesel oil and the thrum of machinery a person indifferent to flora and fauna may be. And as there are about twenty-two genera and well over nine hundred species of *Violaceae* worldwide, it's not surprising that we make strong and personal judgements about these flowers. I know I have written about violets, violas and pansies earlier in the book, including those aberrations, those nightmare mutations bred for show with faces distorted by chrome and purple patches too heavy to remain vertical without support, but now I want to write about the species of this genus: the source of all the hybrids we buy by the fistful each spring and autumn.

Violets have been with us for thousands of years and but for them, and for their continuing existence, we would never have the annual treat of stocking our flower beds from seeds and nurseries with members of this motley clan just as demurely or as flamboyantly as we choose. Lose the wild flowers, and we would lose our source of renewal.

In America, at the end of the last century, New England was the mecca of violet growing and, as in London, violets were sold on the streets of New York. Natives of the violet family, such as *Viola blanda*, are still to be found in the United States from Maine to Georgia. *V. canadensis* is a herb of the eastern seaboard and the Rockies, while a tall, striped viola, *V. striata*, and the large-bloomed Great American Violet, *V. cucullata*, are found in the far north of the continent.

In the Olympic National Park in the state of Washington are found three of the most lovely violas: the hook violet, the pioneer violet and the Flett violet. The hook violet, *V. adunca*, a low, deep blue flower with a white heart, and the tall pioneer violet, *V. glabella*, a brilliant yellow flower with heart-shaped leaves and purple 'honey guides', both grow in the impenetrable forest, where openings of the tree canopy allow enough sunlight through, and also in the subalpine zone (similar to the subarctic regions of Canada), where the growing season is short and where, in midsummer, there are moist meadows and dry hillsides. The hook violet is also widespread in the temperate parts of north America and the pioneer violet is found in southern Alaska and the Sierra Nevada.

The third of these violas is rare: the Flett violet, *V. flettii*, is bluish-purple and only appears in the high country after the last snow has melted among rocky crevices of the peaks on the south and west-facing slopes. The Flett violet is among seven other plants endemic to the area which somehow have clung to life ever since the Pleistocene Ice Age. Glaciers, about three thousand feet deep, left isolated peaks rising above frozen desolation, and where these eight relics have miraculously survived.

The violet family are promiscuous; given the chance, they would inveigle us to sigh over their frailty throughout north European countries and Greenland, the Mediterranean, Asia Minor, the Caucasus, Syria, Palestine and North Africa; on through Kashmir, the Atlas mountains and the Himalayas, to central Siberia and the Altai mountains; and, improbable as it may seem, the marsh violet inhabits the Azores.

For the following information on the thirteen species indigenous to Britain I am unequivocally indebted to a friend and botanist, Jo Dunn. Without her painstaking field work and research as well as her scholarly notes, photographs and patient guidance, I should be wallowing in a sea of violets, unable to disentangle one tiny flower from another.

Here are their Latin names for those in the know or on the brink of becoming that way: *Viola odorata* (sweet violet); *V. hirta* (hairy violet); *V. rupestris* (Teesdale violet); *V. riviniana* (common dog-violet); *V. reichenbachiana* (early dog-violet); *V. canina* (heath dog-violet); *V. lactea* (pale dog-violet); *V. persicifolia* (fen violet); *V. palustris* (marsh violet);

V. lutea (mountain pansy); *V. tricolor* (wild pansy but also known as heartsease); *V. tricolor subspecies curtisii* (dune pansy); *V. arvensis* (field pansy); and *V. kitaibeliana* (dwarf pansy).

Starting with the sweet violet, this one appears early in the year with a span of colour varying from deep purple, through lilac and rosy-mauve to white and it's the only one of our violets which is scented. How surprising when you think how often we associate these flowers with fragrance. The sweet violet lurks; scrub, hedgerows or woodland are its territory as well as chalky soil. In country churchyards where it may occur naturally or may have been deliberately introduced from gardens or countryside, it remains safe from annihilation by the manic use of herbicides which still pollutes even some of our graveyards. As summer progresses reproduction of the sweet violet is either by self-pollination or by means of 'stolons', the surface runners, rather as strawberries take root.

The scentless hairy violet in shades of shadowy blue-violet veined with purple, is as beautiful as any in this country. Found in open, calcareous grassland it is clumpy in growth with a creamy eye and leaves which when young scroll inwards the way some shells are devised. The hairiness comes from the roughness of the leaves and dense hairs on the leaf-stalks which make it easy to distinguish from the sweet violet. Instead of runners, it has seeds and seed-stalks rich in oil. Jo tells me she has found young seed-coats lying in little heaps around these flowers: the work of that nocturnal and big-eared creature, the wood mouse, which has an appetite for juicy fruit and buds, peas and beans, as well, apparently, as for the hairy violet. As for ants, a kind of symbiosis has arisen between them and the violets: because they relish the oily seed-stalks, the ants carry the seeds away, dispersing them among anthills where the plants grow with abundance. Although widespread in Britain, the hairy violet has become so rare in the Burren, County Clare, Ireland, that it is now a protected species.

The third of these native flowers is exquisite. The Teesdale violet is minute: a tufted non-creeper. Hairy all over, it is described as an upland plant and rare in Britain but fortunately it is distributed throughout central Europe including parts of Norway, Corsica, the Italian Alps, Macedonia and Central Asia; in North America from Quebec to Alaska and south from Maine and Oregon. And according to the *Red Data Book*: 'This perennial is known from II localities on open, mossy, sheep-grazed turf or bare ground on limestone in Yorkshire, Durham and Westmorland . . . Though it appears to be adequately protected now, threats exist from collectors, because of its rarity and the proximity of an easy access road in one area, and from the planting of conifers.' (That dreaded habit we have in Britain of spreading sterility up and down our hills.)

Anyone walking country lanes will have seen the common dog-violet, a bluish-violet perennial with a paler spur, concealed on banks or among last year's woodland leaves. It flowers later than the sweet violet and the early dog-violet and, as far as I'm concerned, all three appear impossible to distinguish. But for those in the know, with sharp eyes and the inbuilt habit of looking where they walk, this trio, unless they've hybridized from close proximity, can be sorted out by the shape and colour of the spurs, whether they have runners (which this one hasn't), and from the form of leaves, sepals and stipules.

The fifth in this list is the early dog-violet, another non-creeper distinguished from the common violet by having paler, 'fly-away' petals giving it an alert, listening look. And whereas in the common dog-violet the spur is cream tinged with violet, here the spur is darker than the petals. In England it's everywhere: hedgebanks and woods, on limy or chalky soils, but curiously it is only sprinkled about Wales and Ireland and rare in Scotland.

The heath dog-violet, with short creeping rhizomes, is a very blue species with a yellowish spur, found growing in acid grassland, fens or on heaths.

The seventh flower is enchanting. Milky-coloured and ghostly, this noncommital pale dog-violet has leaves often tinged with purple, adding to its unearthly quality. Growing in scattered localities on dry heaths in Anglesey and Pembroke, Sussex, Essex and often in south-west England, the flower is also found in parts of Ireland. On the Gower peninsula in south Wales Jo Dunn hunted it down on cliff-tops, surprised to find it growing so close to the sea.

The fen violet, *V. persicifolia* (which descriptively means 'with leaves like those of the peach tree' and was called *persica malus* by Pliny), is a beautiful flower a breath away from vanishing. Rare! Endangered! Vulnerable! What other adjectives carry such dire forebodings? The flower, looking as frail as its tenuous fingerhold on life, with hairline veins on the underside of its duck-egg blue petals, a pure white throat, a greenish spur and notched leaves, blooms in May and June in the fens of Cambridgeshire, Huntingdonshire, and among damp grassy hollows on the limestone of western Ireland from Fermanagh to Clare. Hounded from the fens by drainage, chivvied into its one remaining habitat on newly disturbed peat in Huntingdonshire, the fen violet has triumphantly reappeared, after sixty years' absence, among the peat diggings of Cambridgeshire. And in Ireland, because it grows near the turloughs – those strange lakes with fluctuating water levels that lie among limestone rocks – it's known as the turlough violet. Thankfully in other parts of the world this endearing little creeping herb still exists.

The marsh violet has a delicate face. Pale lilac with darker honey guides spread across the petals like a delta, the plant lives up to its squelchy name by perpetuating itself with creeping rhizomes in bogs, marshes, fens and wet heaths.

The next five are pansies. It is impossible not to gush over their expressive faces. 'Adorable' sounds sickening, but that is how they look. Each is as winning as the last. Enjoyment, surprise, alertness, reticence or self-deprecation – they reveal it all.

Though the plants are small – some often skulk among leaves or tufty grasses – differences in appearance and habit make it easy to distinguish the wild pansy from the violets. The latter, which must be painstakingly searched for, are synonymous with modesty, shyness and all those fairly low-key attributes that have long been associated with this flower. And while two of the pansies may be said to possess such qualities, the other three (including a subspecies) – the mountain, wild and dune pansies – though they could never be called immodest, are relatively bolder. As their names suggest, they go in for a more open lifestyle. Although they share with the violet nectar-filled spurs and radiating honey guides on their petals, pansy flowers differ in having flat, more rounded faces which, in most cases, are larger and more vividly coloured; and while pansy leaves aren't dissimilar from those of violets, their stipules are distinctive, being leaf-like and deeply lobed.

If appearance were all, then you only need to look at the beautiful, enquiring face of a bright yellow or violet-coloured mountain pansy to realize that this is where demureness all but vanishes and a hint of showiness begins. No wonder the cultivation of many strains of our garden pansies started here.

The mountain pansy is bright yellow but occasionally, to baffle you, the flat flowers may be purple or blotched, arbitrarily lined with honey guides on its naïve and cheerful face. The flower grows in upland, often calcium-deficient grassland, and on rocky ledges in every county north of a line between the Humber and the Severn.

Some modern garden pansies have evolved from hybrids between this one and heartsease. According to which way you face, show and fancy pansies have been its ultimate fate or triumph.

Now we come to heartsease whose name ought to shower us with blessings. The wild pansy, *V. tricolor*, appears everywhere there are recording enthusiasts, in the garden or in the wild: 'It groweth often among the corne,' wrote William Turner in 1548. And it still does. Deep purple, light mauve, yellow or combinations of these, this flower seeks acid, light or sandy waste ground, or short grassland throughout most of Europe, though rarely in the south and then only on mountains. Judging by the long list of local names with love and kiss in them, this plant provokes particularly endearing associations. To name a few: Love-in-Idleness, Leap-up-and-Kiss-Me and Kiss-Me-Love-at-the-Garden-Gate speak of a rural idyll well suited to a retiring flower known as heartsease. Oberon, in *A Midsummer Night's Dream*, squeezed the juice from Love-in-Idleness into the eye of Titania so that on waking she would fall in love with Bottom. Why it should have so many love names is not clear, but in contrast to this jolly wantonness the herb also has a pious image: thought by some to have the appearance of three faces under a hood, it is also known as '*Trinitatis herba*' – the Blessed Trinity flower.

Among the monumental range of research undertaken by Darwin during his long lifetime (which included a study of the life cycle of earthworms), he studied the way transplanted heartsease so instantly changed colour and markings, and yet could return to their original colours before the end of the summer. Such capriciousness was a bane and a boon. In the wild, in different soil and climatic conditions, identifying *Viola* species could become very hit-and-miss. On the other hand heartsease, with agreeable facility, could breed a whole chiaroscuro of offspring. The violet family are apt to lose their heads when it comes to procreation, and cross-breed avidly, which accounts for the numerous progeny of pretty hybrids that turn up in our gardens, their parentage unrecorded until it is too late for the botanist intent on nomenclature. Even in the gardens of Buckingham Palace, Dr David Bellamy has discovered three vagrants: the common dog-violet, the field pansy and, let's hope it works, heartsease.

The dune pansy (*V.* subsp. *curtisii*), is almost like a small mountain pansy. Yellow, blue-violet or parti-coloured, this perennial has flowers with such stand-up petals it has a prick-eared expression which is most appealing. By adapting to inhospitable terrain it grows in dunes and grassy places close to the sea in parts of Britain, as well as the chilly shores of the Baltic.

The twelfth and most self-effacing of the lot is the field pansy. Usually a yellow as pale as clotted cream, this annual is commonly found on cultivated or waste ground in Europe or as remotely far flung as in Siberia, Iran, Iraq and north Africa. 'This is one of the arable "weeds" which has resisted elimination by modern herbicides,' says Jo Dunn. 'When the capsules explode, the seeds may be spread as far as two metres.' Luckily these tactics help to ensure that the plant survives. But only those partial to bending over as they walk the countryside would have the engrossed patience to notice the flower as Jo does. As she succinctly remarks: 'It's a small, rather over-looked pansy, which needs to have a hand-lens focused on its face before it can be appreciated!'

The last of this tribe is the dwarf pansy: a very rare annual with a hooded cream or pale violet face, its flower is minute, sometimes no more than one inch in height, but it has great charm. Jo Dunn admits she has only seen this pansy once, by crawling on hands and knees with a lens at the ready: 'I marvelled that anything so small could survive!' Survive it does, just, on the dunes of the Scilly and Channel Islands and, according to the ominous and somewhat puzzling words of the *Red Data Book*, it 'will be endangered only if digging for sand ceases and rabbits become extinct'. For unlike so many wild and garden plants – it thrives on disturbance.

Whether grown from seed or by division the full range of *Violaceae* for the garden means you have your hands on an infinity of variations. Their colour range is past defining; so many of the species of *Viola* from all over the world, not just the thirteen I've listed here, have produced superb cultivars. And for those gardeners hankering to trace long-forgotten flowers, David Stuart and James Sutherland have a nursery in Scotland, 'Plants from the Past', which lists a wonderful collection.

Once, inspired by a floral design made from pots of petunias and marigolds that I'd seen in Rajasthan, I tried to repeat the same thing with pinks and pansies. The pots there had been arranged in rising concentric circles, their flamboyant splendour throbbing with vibrancy, half in and half out of the shade of citrus trees. The effect was prodigal and spectacular, with the luxuriance of jewellery glowing in the shadows.

Having neither the space nor an inexhaustible supply of Indian labour, I made only one sphere. I copied their idea of using upturned pots arranged in circular rising tiers of height, and stood my pots of flowers to form a closely textured dome. They looked sumptuous; pansies the colour of aubergines and indigo, draining into mauve and amethyst, surmounted by blue and steel, sparingly highlighted by marbled pinks. The problem was space; I had not allowed enough. Nor was our pastoral garden, full of globular and disorderly roses, the setting for something so architecturally peerless. But for anyone wanting to try this idea, remember! You must be able to stand back, to walk around, to look from all sides and at different hours of the day, so as to see how the light falls on the petals – a sight unbelievably voluptuous and hedonistic.

CHAPTER VIII

THE LAST SERENE FRONTIER
Autumn

ON'T CARRY AWAY THAT ARM TILL I HAVE TAKEN OFF my ring,' ordered Lord Raglan after his arm had been amputated. Now I call that fortitude, which is what many gardeners need when the days are shortening and the acrid smell of bonfires fills the air rather than the fragrance of lilies.

By November the wind blows with a chill from the north and I seek the warmth and comforting smell of Boots the chemist rather than the sludgy amalgam of decaying leaves underfoot. A sense of security hovers round the Women's Institute cake stall, attended by ladies in flowery pinnies as solicitous as nannies; light shining from the Jubilee Hall casts a beneficent light on shoppers hurrying back to tea; and I am assuaged by notes from the cashpoint machine, which always come out warm as if on the other side someone's hand had been waiting for me.

This is the time of year for lit rooms at dusk. I used to linger over the chapter in *The Wind in the Willows* in which lost, homesick and frightened, Mole looks wistfully at the 'squares of a dusky orange-red on either side of the street, where the firelight or lamplight of each cottage overflowed through the casements into the dark world without'. The description evoked an instantaneous image of late autumn when in town or country an overwhelming despondency from the gilded wreckage of trees is a season when champions for spring feel abandoned.

Few things perish like a garden with its own particular technicolour lucidity from copper and buttery leaves; unlike rotting food, or lines on the face, a garden goes out in triumphal fluorescence laced with a sweet sense of melancholy. A transforming light engulfs the evening as a spectral moon brings apprehension for the first signs of frost, and on early mornings footprints mark the lawn; garden chairs are folded away and the once rose-clad loggia is full of unswept leaves. By late autumn my enthusiasm for gardening is curling at the edges as I look forward to the impassive oblivion of winter.

There is no right way of making a garden, axiomatic and foolproof, only alternatives. Yet we are brain-washed into thinking there is. Certain professionals put the wind up us: they speak authoritatively, particularly on television or in magazines, and in the end banal gardening is absorbed through the process of osmosis; patio, trough or trellis will be planted with deadly over-nicety and the garden will lack innovation. Unbelievably, new gardeners are still being faced towards the wavy-edged flower beds on either side of the mandatory lawn, and the trio of blue, columnar and prostrate conifers as background to the patio and its polystyrene Greek urns. Garden clichés breed like greenfly. Only recently a well-known and long-established nursery was putting out a design for the front gardens on a new housing estate, without an iota of sensitivity and of such unmitigated ugliness that it bore no relationship to the spirit of a garden.

How far we have regressed since generations ago Francis Bacon wrote at the beginning of the seventeenth century: 'And because the breath of flowers is far sweeter in the air (where it comes and goes, like the warbling of music) than in the hand, therefore nothing is more fit for that delight, than to know what be the flowers and plants that do best perfume the air.' (Bacon had been a student at Trinity College, Cambridge, at the precocious age of thirteen, leaving, according to Macaulay, after three years, with contempt for the place and the apposite conviction that 'the system of academic education in England was radically vicious . . .')

He dismisses as having little scent rosemary, bay and sweet marjoram, but extols violets, 'especially the white double violet, which comes twice a year, about the middle of April, and about Bartholomew-tide'. Others listed for their scent include strawberry leaves as they die, and less idiosyncratically, wallflowers, pinks and honeysuckles. 'But those which perfume the air most delightfully, not passed by as the rest, but being trodden upon and crushed, are three: that is, burnet, wild thyme, and water mints . . . to have the pleasure when you walk or tread.'

Now fast-forward and return to the 1990s: you will find among the gems recommended by the nursery for the charming enhancement of housing-estate gardens – conifers, alpines and heathers.

Defect! Behave dangerously! Garden pundits should be catalysts provoking the raw gardener to seek alternatives; to get away from the freeze/cook approach to making a garden. Eclectic stimuli should be thrown at his feet like challenging gloves. Why not go in for floral mutiny? Chuck out tastefulness, decorum, restraint, moderation and protocol and be outrageous with red hot pokers. Have a field-day with acanthus and toss caution to the wind with gentians whose azure flowers transfix the eye of the garden as emphatically as a butterfly is impaled in the Natural History Museum.

Are cushions left unplumped or an abandoned book lying spread-eagled on the arm of a chair signs of chronic degeneracy? Why should dust on the furniture be condemned when bloom on a plum is esteemed? Are daisies in the lawn really the end of a gardener's world, proving conclusively a loss of control? It's only an attitude of mind. Gertrude Jekyll, that myopic lady who has influenced our garden plantings through the years, added Caucasian giant hogweed to her borders, though nowadays along with Japanese knotweed and Himalayan

131

balsam, it's considered a marauding hooligan and is banned from our gardens. But in the innocent days of Jekylldom giant hogweed made an imposing statement at the entrance to her paths or steps; they may have been considered coarse, but Miss Jekyll knew exactly what dominance the plants achieved in unexpected places.

Why aren't we emboldened to plant down the middle of a garden rather than round the edges? Or to have paths running along boundaries covered with scrambling climbers, instead of making a path as a spine with curvature running dead centre towards a rockery? Why not put tall airy flowers in front of smaller ones? And old hands at gardening should be pointing out the relationship which exists between fern and pebble; inert solids and organic effervescence; flights of steps and crumpled leaves. Even a concrete paving slab may have its moment.

Recently I met a woman so intimidated that her instinct to be deviant and to wander from the norm was crushed by what her neighbours might think. Newly widowed, she was overwhelmed by the grass-mowing which her husband had undertaken with such pride. She admitted that throughout the summer she was kept awake by worry over how to cope with her husband's legacy – the lawn. But there isn't an archetypal garden design, a kind of omnipotent blueprint, which must be adhered to. She yearned to do away with grass altogether and in its place to lay down paving and plant easily-maintained scented shrubs, but guilt and fear of being condemned as feckless by those on either side of her, whose lawns and borders were as titivated as flower arrangements laid out before judges, kept her compliant. What she needed was encouragement; a few seditionist voices urging her to be bold and oust the lawn; nudging her gently in the direction her instinct was telling her to go rather than struggling to keep the grass as closely shaved as pile on a carpet.

The last I heard, she was still mowing.

Controlled wilderness is hard work. Careless gardening is not what it seems. To begin with it's not careless. Cow parsley wasn't in our garden through negligence but because, when sitting by the stream, we wanted to see the brazenly pink rose, 'Zéphirine Drouhin', through the creamy lace of the flowers. The whole choreography of our garden meant that keeping it to the right degree of wilderness needed stern application; the line between harmony and disintegration is a fine one. Our method of gardening appeared haphazard, with the tulips growing among long grass, but the flounces of the roses trailing on the ground kept us in bondage all summer long, needing to sickle round the frilly bits before nettles and grass obliterated their hems. It was arduous; mowing became a co-operative obligation, when I would hoist up the straggles of roses on the prongs of a hay fork while Michael pushed the mower beneath.

The tumbled disarray which some of our best gardeners achieve, with what looks like artless genius, has form. Ask them, and they admit that those parts of the garden which look so spontaneous need painstaking attention, defined and inspired.

Being alone in a garden never feels solitary but being alone in New York is to feel marooned. Three years ago I was there in mid March, partly to see friends and publishers but also to visit the Philadelphia Flower Show. Through the generosity of friends of friends I'd been lent a flat in Manhattan and if I'd had a companion with me we would have sailed headlong into the city where clouds are reflected in the sides of buildings and hot blasts rise up between underground grating like a breath from hell.

The apartment was not as I had expected. Once off the street I entered a silence so oppressive it felt tangible; not a murmur came from traffic at the end of the block. Was I alone or did others inhabit the building? But travel is bracing stuff: I walked up dimly-lit stairs past doors where, if anyone's eye was at the peephole, I was unaware. Not until I reached the top floor was there a sign of occupation: outside one of the doors was a collection of discarded shoes littering the threshold, shoes which, each time I returned, had been redistributed, flung with wanton casualness as though the owner couldn't wait to get through the door.

The apartment, frayed, seedy and soiled, with book shelves of wonderful old English editions, with photographs, pictures, crucifixes, knick-knacks and grey bedding, ran from front to back of the building, allowing me to look down onto the street on one side or have a back view of the building in the next block. Between us was a concrete yard in which grew one tree in whose leafless branches, miraculously, as though placed there by some celestial humorist and the only colour in that dismal vault, was a green balloon. Its string had anchored it to the tree like a bauble, vibrant and living, in a drab waste of asphalt.

Only later I noticed the fire escape outside the kitchen window: a rusty cobweb, it clung to the building by bolts as fragile as skeletal fingers. Anyone using this method of escape would take their life in their hands. The flight of steps would instantly detach itself from the wall and sway towards the arms of the tree and the beckoning viridescence of a stranded balloon.

Daytime was fine, and anyway I was mostly out, but by evening I began to feel removed from reality. This detached feeling was partly due to the curtainless windows; as darkness fell a few lights appeared across the street, which only emphasized the sense of suspended unreality as though I were living on a Woody Allen set. The first night my bare toes felt indescribable textures and nameless things under the bed. I didn't stoop to look; like the fridge and kitchen cupboard, they were better left unobserved, and every night after that I went to bed in socks.

Light in the sitting-room was supplied by a bulb growing like a malignant growth from the back of a ceramic pig. Pig ornaments abounded and as I have loved pigs ever since we had our own sow, Honey, I was enchanted by the ingenuity of stuffed pigs, piggy cushions,

porkish pictures and porcine ashtrays. In the kitchen and bathroom the unshaded lights worked by pulling on pieces of string blackened by years of use; the bathroom, whose window was covered by a scrap of grey material, had no basin, which meant teeth-cleaning was done over the kitchen sink where the drain gave off a stench as though from the putrefying intestines deep in the guts of Cerberus. (Curious: in the morning the mug I had used was full of small black insects.) Under the bath was a trayful of seasoned cat litter and over the bath, suspended from the ceiling, a giant croissant the size of a life belt.

Only when David Wheeler, whose gardening journal *Hortus* is widely read in America, came to stay for a couple of nights, did the apartment shed its baleful mood. Then its personality revived; everything hung out; unlike so many kitchens where nothing showed what the room was used for, where every item of food, every utensil was hidden away as though prepared for surgery. When David and I went to the nearest grocery and brought back food and drink, the silence of the stairway was a benison promising privacy and a shared cosiness from eating dinner surrounded by pigs.

I may sound sanguine now, unfazed by living in this apartment, but it wasn't quite like that. Far from it; one night when someone rang my bell and I knew the intercom between flat and doorstep didn't work, imagining it was David unexpectedly returned, I thoughtlessly released the front door lock. No one appeared. I watched through the spy-hole, listening for a footstep on the stairs, until panic overcame me and I thought I couldn't sleep there another night. I got as far as looking up hotels in the telephone directory until I realized there was no way out (no, not the fire escape) except by those dimly-lit stairs where the stranger I had let in might still be lurking. The thought was more menacing than staying put. I gave up thoughts of hotel foyers, of rooms connected by phone to the receptionist, and by morning, early, I could hear the soothing coo of pigeons in the tree outside the window.

We lived in a world of scintillating contrasts. One day, lunching with a publisher, we sat in a restaurant where outside the window there were skaters in their woolly clothes twirling and gliding as we ate clam chowder and walnut rolls, and sliced oranges in mint decorated with pansies dusted with sugar.

As for the Flower Show in Philadelphia it was so flauntingly spectacular that it put in the shade any bed of annuals at a roundabout

in Geneva. 'Olé!' announced the Spanish garden display. 'Will you look at that elegance!' exclaimed a visitor in front of a wedding table festooned with satin bows, bouquets and three-foot purple candles encircled by flowers. 'Isn't that neat!' cried another, discovering pansies between flagstones. The enthusiasm, friendliness and warmth of colour lapped around me so that for a few hours I quite forgot I should be returning to the spooky apartment in New York that night.

During my week in New York David and I went to visit the garden and glasshouses at Wave Hill, where the curator, Marco Polo Stufano, welcomed us with effervescent enthusiasm. Wave Hill at that time of the year was unbelievably beautiful. Its setting, on the rim of New York city, made the contents of the alpine house seem fabulous, I really do mean 'fabulous', set down among the snow and desolate river banks of the Hudson.

We also went to Long Island. Although in England bulbs and sprigs of green were on the move, here there wasn't a vestige of spring; the grass was brown, as desiccated as in Greece at the end of summer. I shouldn't have been surprised, but until then I hadn't realized just how withering and bleak the soil was in that part of the country, and how short the spring must be, when there wasn't even a spear of daffodil thrusting up through the earth. There can be no subtlety about the arrival of spring; no coquettish ripening or arousal of bud; no lingering over primroses when the protracted season moves forward in stealthy green revelations; but instead, apparently, there comes a day in April when: 'Bare winter suddenly was changed to spring.' Gardening here would have more constraints on timing than anything I faced at home. It was on Long Island too, that the foreignness of the country was again brought home to me. That evening at dinner, my neighbour who had been talking about books looked at me and announced out of the blue: 'Shoot the mustard!' Nonplussed, I wasn't sure if it was a threat or a directive.

The kindness and hospitality from people David and I met was in sharp contrast to the impersonality of New York, where 'everybody pass you by like a freight train pass a hobo' as a gardener in the Midwest once said. And it was further enhanced next day when I took a bus named the 'Hampton Jitney' back to New York. Instead of being impersonal, it turned out to be so chummy that everyone seemed an old habitué. Our hostess offered us newspapers, coffee or cold drinks, gossiped with the passengers, and as we progressed she directed the driver exactly where each person wanted to alight. At one point in Manhattan someone came aboard to ask if anyone had seen her husband. He'd got off the stop before, people told her. It was more like the old country bus which used

138

to travel the lanes of Shropshire, where a shopping bag left on the verge showed that a passenger was filling in time by having a cup of tea in the nearest cottage, than a bus negotiating the streets of Manhattan. The 'Hampton Jitney' went to my heart as did the man on 2nd Avenue whom I stopped to ask what a letterbox looked like; having directed me to a drab green-grey contraption covered in graffiti, he turned back to help when he saw me groping for the handle to the concealed opening.

American gardens are my Mecca. I long to see them whether their owners are collaborating with nature among the high altitudes of Idaho or the prairies of Wisconsin, or are conquering the desert landscape of New Mexico where I imagine there are bizarre plants as alien to me as hummingbirds. But whether it is sandy loam or blue-black soil, why do American gardeners denigrate the earth, the precious stuff on which they are dependent for all their floral effects and fantasies, so dismissively as 'dirt'? Just as I find it strange that small gardens are called 'yards', which conjure up for me confined places housing dustbins and bicycles, empty wine bottles and discarded plant containers.

One of the incentives for visiting American gardens, apart from the obvious diversity of climate and terrain, is the correspondence I have had with gardeners from different parts of the country. In response to my book *A Gentle Plea for Chaos*, people have written letters describing their own gardens and often including photographs. A lady from Ohio wrote of her green garden full of spring bulbs, yuccas and lilies, which is entirely enclosed by fir trees among which she loves to walk in winter for nothing more than the pleasure of their murky shade. Another correspondent had gardened in southern California for twenty years, where disaster followed disaster with her primulas, hepaticas, trilliums and lilacs until she acquiesced and had to put up with hibiscus, camellias, epiphyllum and jacarandas.

Photographs from an Oregon enthusiast show a small garden literally hewn out of a dark forest, where foxgloves and Californian poppies rampage. One letter writer, living sixty miles from New York, made a formal garden around the family's nineteenth-century farmhouse, but then allowed pinks, corydalis and roses to spill over boundaries with lackadaisical abandon while she sat enjoying the place with an unperturbed passion. There were so many of these gardeners: people pioneering, unflagging, stubborn or bewitched by what they were growing, whatever the climate or altitude, who took the trouble to write about a part of their lives which was private and stirring, irrational and loved.

And then there are Australian gardeners.

The letters I had from some of them bowled me over; not only for their energy and their mettle but for their descriptions of a climate so savage and violent it made me realize that Michael and I had been gardening in paradise. Theirs were some of the most anguished letters I received. Locusts, snakes, drought, bush fires and scorching winds off the desert meant continual strife. Taming the wilderness, resiting boulders, and yet trying to keep the garden integrated with the overpowering and starkly beautiful bush just beyond the boundary, was their lodestar. No mild curiosity plucked at their subconscious until they felt provoked to cultivate a few sweet williams. Theirs was no gentle philandering. Their gardening came from a flame in the gut, from a hunger for flowers, a longing for trees, a kind of cupidity – not for fame, but to wrest one calm eye out of their wolfish surroundings.

From Western Australia, where obviously the writer was not so menaced as some, a gardener wrote describing his lemon-scented eucalypts flanking the drive, where flame trees and cypress pines grow above camellias, azaleas and rhododendrons in a garden where he also grew passion fruit, citrus, avocado, loquats and 'monstera deliciosa', as

well as gardenias, wattle and magnolias, and three ninety-year-old trees: a jacaranda, a carob and an olive. 'At one time I had thought of making it a Japanese garden, all sparse and significant . . .' Fortunately, he didn't. A man in Queensland, in the midst of luxuriant greenery, revealed his secret longings: 'the epitome of luxury would be to have a bed on rails which would roll out onto a tree-top platform on fine mornings among the orchids and the honeyeaters . . .'

From New South Wales one young gardener who had written about her frustration over her garden, replied to my query as to why didn't she stick to the indigenous plants, with a trenchant answer: 'I haven't yet been converted to the school of Australian natives – they are the most difficult things to grow (anyway all our fertilizing and composting has made the soil too rich for these plants with their negligible nutritional needs), at the same time I have lost my craving for perennial borders and for flowers that only bloom in the middle of summer. Summer is when we're locked indoors with the air-conditioner at full blast.' The summer she was referring to was 43 degrees centigrade for days on end.

Gardening in those conditions? We can't be speaking the same language. Her account left me gasping, not from heat but from the thought of the insurmountable enemy. Yet, undaunted, and using her irrigation system once a week, she was hoping for the best. 'Today I noted the golden ash was in flower with a million bees buzzing all over it . . . last week we had an inch of rain producing a glimmer of green on the hills. I managed to rush out and plant 25 trees.' Among them were *Gleditsia triacanthos*, *Brachychiton populneus*, *Fraxinus oxycarpa*, *Celtis occidentalis* and the local she-oak, *Casuarina cunninghamiana*, which makes an eerie sound as the wind blows through; *Populus* x *canadensis* 'Aurea', *Ulmus chinensis*, a variety of *Melaleuca* and 'a handful of different eucalypts', as well as two English oaks she'd grown from acorns.

'A pathetic effort really in a barren hundred-acre paddock.' Pathetic? I call it both heroic and stoic. 'The idea,' she wrote, 'was to have a grand planting I could see from the top balcony of the house. I wanted autumnal colours of green greens – not just the grey dull shades of the local species we have all around . . . but the hot winds make a mockery of rain. The black soil is cracked . . . our little bit of irrigation producing a meagre oasis.' Her soulful words rang like a cry from the heart: 'All that energy and time for a tiny patch of green amidst rolling hills that, in the last few months, have taken on the colour of sand dunes!'

She-oaks ('dwarf sheoke'; casuarinas), with no leaves but slender bamboo-like stems, apparently brown off when in flower and from a distance look as though they are going to die, so that the Forestry

Commission, inundated by anxious callers, have a recorded message at a certain time in the year, reassuring gardeners that the casuarinas are merely changing colour. 'I loathed the she-oaks to begin with. However after looking at them for five years I've come to adore them. They serve the same garden purpose as a European pine does for you northerners.'

Near to where this gardener and her family live is a hidden hillside covered with the extraordinary *Xanthorrhoea australis*, the slow-growing grass-tree said to be a thousand years old, with clumps of long, brittle, very thin leaves growing straight from the trunk. 'We discovered the valley (we call it our Valley of the Dinosaurs) in autumn when the wattle was a blaze of gold. The new spears of the grass trees were just being held aloft covered with buds about to flower . . . finding thousands of them is so remarkable I can't bring myself to uproot any for the garden. Their place is in the hills.' Finally, as if to really bring it home to me what gardening in her part of the country means, she wrote in reference to the bit in my book where I describe the way Michael used to cut winding paths through the long grass in the orchard: 'Oh, how I wish we could! But in a country that's home to eleven of the most venomous snakes in the world, that's out of the question.' One day, seeing a deadly six-foot brown snake heading for the back door, she 'shot it with a gun I keep in the laundry'.

What on earth am I whingeing about? Slugs.

One last word on Australian gardens as an antidote to gardening in the bush: a correspondent from Sydney described her hundred-foot garden as having 'a sort of Tuscan courtyard off the kitchen with its walls laced with ivy . . . ' A slab of sandstone, flanked by two columns from Rajasthan, leads down to the garden. And then, as if that weren't improbable enough, she added: 'We are overshadowed by a huge jacaranda tree and three robinias which grow inside [*sic*] our garage and right out through the roof creating a cathedral of leaves.' I love the idea; I envy the dashing and sensational picture her description evokes.

I've never been to South America but I felt lured there when I read a few years ago that scientists drilling boreholes off the coast of Peru found microbes which last saw the light of day roughly three million years ago. Young, compared to a ginkgo tree, I know, but facts so stunning my thoughts can only boggle in disbelief. (Since they found the microbes, have they incubated them in a laboratory, I wonder?)

Facts like these are compelling. They mostly sound like wild-eyed random fantasies thought up by over-active imaginations. Implausible. Embellished; but so sensational they have a sobering influence when the garden, or someone, is getting out of hand. When I read that the Hubble Space Telescope was built to focus on galaxies fifty million light years distant, it did bring me down to earth pretty sharpish. The 'ultimate power source is thought to be a supermassive black hole accreting matter at its heart'. To an ignoramus this is heady stuff, the breath of life; and, come to think of it, I'm not sure that some of us haven't been accreting matter to our hearts for years.

CHAPTER IX

THE STATUE WITHIN THE ROCK
Time

F RANCIS BACON IN HIS ESSAY ON GARDENS WROTE: 'God Almighty first planted a garden. And indeed it is the purest of human pleasures . . . the greatest refreshment to the spirits of man; without which, buildings and palaces are but gross handyworks . . .' The fact that Bacon was writing about princely gardens of not less than thirty acres does not diminish his basic tenet.

His ideal would be for four acres 'assigned to the green; six to the heath; four and four to either side; and twelve to the main garden'. The detail delights me with its extravagance, decoration and intemperate capriciousness. For instance: 'over every arch, a little turret, with a belly, enough to receive a cage of birds; and over every space between the arches some other little figure, with broad plates of round coloured glass, gilt, for the sun to play upon'. He then continues to specify with fascinating precision and verve how he visualizes the banks and alleys, the hedges and the vistas from the 'hither end'. Anyone who gardens should read his essay for his fervent enthusiasm for unruly places such as thickets made only from 'sweet-briar and honeysuckle, and some wild vine . . .'. 'I like also little heaps, in the nature of mole-hills . . . to be set, some with wild thyme; some with pinks; some with germander . . .'; and on and on he goes, singing about periwinkles, violets, cowslips, daisies, lilies, roses and sweet williams.

I really don't have much sympathy for the perpetuation nor the recreation of a garden once the owner is dead. However fastidiously the original is adhered to, some spirited vitality will be missing. Like an artist copying an old master, the high tension won't be there. Why not make something else instead of painstakingly following in Miss Jekyll's booted footsteps? Even though they persevere, those who attempt it will never reincarnate her garden with its own artistry, its own voice and presiding spirit. And yet, after having read Francis Bacon and after being so opinionated as to banish in one fell swoop all those dedicated disciples of dead gardeners, I can't help thinking what fun it would be, given thirty acres of 'set aside' farming land and a blank cheque, to take on Bacon's ideal garden.

From following his design, his advice on how the folds of the land should be contrived, by noting his specific instructions for shade and shelter, and by taking to heart his sense of atmosphere, could we re-create a kind of pastiche of his ideal seventeenth-century garden? He is authoritarian: for instance when planting fruit trees within borders of flowers he advises the flowers should be used sparingly, 'lest they deceive the trees'. His essay is full of delightful phrases like this; dogmatic opinions, precise instructions, are sprinkled through the text and his bouncy spirit comes across with heart-warming empathy. In the end his mood is so contagious that the three hundred or so years which divide us are concertinaed, as we share with him those same visions we each have for making a garden into an ultimate floral paradise.

Coming down to earth, not even thinking in Baconish terms, I remember how I felt when I first gardened. I was trigger-happy. Fast movers, foolproof foliage and punctual flowers were what I was after. Oniy later did I become aware how, surreptitiously, the early frenzy had dissolved and how, quite unbeknown to me, my whole ethos had somersaulted. Now my garden lies like a calm oasis; passive and potential. It is up to me as to how I set about its flowering. What is me, shows: the design I go for, the plants I choose, the way I tend them – is mine. I need make no allowances. But beware! I know full well that at the very moment I think I am in control, when I complacently imagine that it is my hand which pulls the string, it is then that the garden starts to control me. So, though I am the one to make the decisions as to what to plant and what not to, each shrub I have put into my present garden only adds to my thraldom. I'm not complaining – just stating.

The garden and I have a relationship which means that, the longer it goes on the more I surround myself with mental space and, should I want it, self-discovery. But then emptying the mind in preparation for this great self-centred revelation presupposes I had something there in the first place. I think I'll pause for a bit, and ponder on that one.

I am sitting in sunlight in my garden. I have come here, abandoning my word processor, for the chance of being passively receptive to this actual moment when the morning is suspended and a few self-sown and obstreperously scarlet poppies are eyeing the sun. A skein of ducks, like a dark streamer, has passed overhead. And although I'm living in a town of around eight thousand people, when the wind blows from the south I hear the lowing of cattle. The river Teme after last night's rain is also audible; so is that call, strident and presumptive, of a cock crowing, a sound so redolent of childhood visits to the country it instantly brings back the June light of early mornings when my sister and I would lean out of the window, long before the household was awake, and plot whether to harass the farmer next door or lose ourselves among the leafy beech woods of Buckinghamshire. Alas, the crowing of a rooster is as rare nowadays as the sight of grasshoppers or glow-worms.

Slowly we are coming to our senses: though we have lost the commonplace sound and sight of cockerels, grasshoppers and glow-worms, we are waking up to how vulnerable these creatures are and how insidious is their disappearance. Naturalists do keep warning those who

are responsible for their
destruction just how many
animals, insects and wild
flowers are under threat.

Where are the starfish,
crabs and lustrous sea
anemones we used to find
in pools after the tide had receded? Where are the monk seals and
iridescent parrot fish of the Mediterranean? Their withdrawal from
our sight has been so underhand that their absence is barely perceptible
until something jogs the memory. And what flowers, small and
undramatic, have all but vanished in the last thirty years? The orchid,
field scabious, snake's head fritillary and wood anemone, for instance:
inconspicuous, undemonstrative, sometimes scentless – what is it about
these flowers? Where does their attraction lie? Why should we peer,
grope and stoop with reverential devotion to seek out the violet? Why is
it imperative that we should preserve them in our islands and feel

trepidation on reading that such little things, so flimsy and inoffensive as the pale violet or dwarf pansy, are under threat when so many greater, more dramatic disasters are looming on the horizon? But it's their impeccable origins, their very defencelessness and fragile deportment and their artless beauty that makes these violets priceless. What hope for us if, because of their chaste demeanour, we neglect their survival? To cold-shoulder a doomed violet may be, in a small way, to become a diminished human being.

Lichens, which live at the extremes of climate from glaciers to the baking roofs of southern France, have taken refuge from toxicity in churchyards, where as many as a hundred different varieties may now find sanctuary. (Memo to the dead: polished granite headstones are useless. Even marble can act as host to algae, but nothing worthwhile latches on to the shiny surface of granite.) Lichens act not only as a kind of pollution barometer, establishing the quality of the air, but as saviours; they are environmental lifelines which set off a whole chain of resurgence.

After an eruption of Mount Vesuvius it needs only a fragment of the greenish-yellow lichen (*Stereocaulon vesuvianum*) to set the whole cycle of regeneration to work, culminating in the slopes eventually being once more cultivated for vines. On the volcanic deposits mountain lichen is succeeded by the spores of moss, then by annual and perennial plants, followed by a yellow bloom from the pea-like blossom of broom; in the end woody common vine is again scrambling over rocks and in time even the evergreen oaks will have taken root.

Usually I work indoors and if the day is fine I try to ignore the sunlight by half drawing the curtains and keeping my eyes on the screen of my machine. Today is different. I have taken some paper and a pen into the garden where I'm sitting at a table made from a slab of slate which came from a men's urinal in the Corvedale. The man who cut it was pleased

enough to have engraved his name and date, the '19th of August 1910' on the slate, and though it had originally served a quite different purpose, I like its matt grey surface to work on and Pooter, the cat, does too. She lies purring beside me from the warmth of the sun which the table has absorbed.

There is no doubt that 'flower power' has meaning which reaches way beyond Haight-Ashbury and the 1960s. If you deny this, you miss out on a major intrinsicality of gardens when a flower is nothing but itself – a flower; it's neither a botanical specimen, nor an outward sign of the gardener's adroitness, nor a symbol for something other than what it is.

Slackness and musing, sensing and vacancy are a great bulk of gardening. Or they should be. Solitude, even if for only a few hours, does allow time for passive regeneration, and if it's possible to reach total receptivity, when the mind is truly vacant and even those tenacious parasites, guilt and fear, can be evicted, I suppose I might reach some sort of contemplative stasis.

The need for temporary solitude is so intense it amounts to an impediment, a malady, chronic and incurable like recurring malaria, which does not afflict everyone. There are many who thrive on hugger-muggerness; who are generous and gregarious, who have a fund of givingness and who welcome taps on the door. But for those whose Plimsoll line for solitude is crucial, is almost palpable, and as necessary as air, they will know what I mean. Like a remittent fever it is nothing you can banish. Outwardly we look okay, but inwardly we are desperate; gasping and frantic for something as integral to ourselves as the colour of our eyes.

Once, after a particularly claustrophobic, stressful and over-populated time when there hadn't been air or space to escape to, suddenly, for a few days, I was alone. It was like emigrating to another planet (in fact I was at home), I just could not believe what had happened. Who was this person I was living with, this stranger, this reasonable, serene foreigner in the house: a becalmed woman who spent her time inwardly humming? The fact that it was myself had no relevance. I was in the company of an alien who moved from room to room with a beneficent composure and totally unfamiliar poise.

My idea of heaven is opening a door into an empty room — not forever, I haven't enough resources, but for at least great chunks of time each day. Anyone who has walked into a garden and seen a distant group of unoccupied chairs as the ultimate comfort will know what I mean. A room or a garden — it doesn't matter which: vacancy is the breath of life, not just for physical solitude but for vacuity of the mind. Gardening provides that no-man's-land where neither small talk nor emotion need intrude. Unfortunately privacy is on the wane; at the best of times it has always been an elusive commodity.

When forty years ago four of us went on a long camping journey, my one imagined necessity I wanted to take with me was a door hanging in its frame. Closing the door behind me as I walked through it, whether in the Savoie or the Anatolian wilderness, although the whole contraption would be standing there alone surrounded by scrub and the small nosy prairie rats which kept popping up and then vanishing, seemed essential if I was to restore my equilibrium. Even on a desert island a framed door would serve a purpose: closing a door behind me has far more vibrant repercussions than the actual physical gesture of pulling the handle to. Just as it has when pushing it open.

At times in my childhood I used to ride a pony, borrowed for the holidays, bareback into the sea. With only a rope halter as harness we plunged into the water until it seemed the pony was afloat; its tail streamed out behind like some sort of undulating seaweed and its mane folded and refolded from the lapping of the water. My legs would float off its flanks until I slowly slipped into the sea, and we would then, with intuitive unanimity, turn back to the shore together. The sense of the sea's strength, the animal's vitality and my own joy for freedom used sometimes to be so intense I felt for a fragmentary second that time stood still and there was neither past nor present. Later we galloped ourselves dry along the wide and empty beach.

That same sense of solitary freedom was recaptured years later when I rode into the jungle on a horse borrowed from a Thai military camp about twelve miles from the northern capital, Chiang Mai. My horse was a huge lumbering creature imported by the army from Australia, hard-mouthed, used for transport not riding – not a beast of great charm, but it did allow me to see parts of the country I could never have reached on foot.

For hours I wandered along earthy tracks through streams and through the forest without meeting anyone. It was not an area of dense jungle. In small clearings I occasionally came across a ramshackle hut on stilts made from woven bamboo with a roof of overlapping teak leaves, surrounded by a few banana trees and several rows of maize. This was not rice-growing territory; the people who lived here survived on the margins of poverty, on a basic economy, growing their own food and weaving their own clothes. The forest men were small, wearing coarsely woven, dark blue cotton shirts and trousers which hung loosely on their lean bodies; the old women, one of whom would invariably be rocking a baby in a cloth hammock, were equally lean, with blackened teeth and red lips from chewing betel nut. The younger women smoked untidily rolled cigars which left such an acrid smell in the air I could always tell when someone had passed along the path long before me. They would look up as I rode by and ask me, with an indifferent curiosity, where I was going and why, in an almost unintelligible dialect.

Huge and brilliant butterflies languidly flew among the trees and whatever the time of year there would always be something in flower. Most spectacular was the 'Coral Tree' when, in the hot season, its waxen pea-shaped flowers formed vermilion racemes among the mostly leafless trees of the forest. Too hot for anything but a leisurely amble, I rode silently except for the crackle under the horse's hooves from large teak leaves which looked from a distance like stones lying in my path.

Occasionally a snake slithered into the dry undergrowth and some-times, if I were lucky, I'd catch sight of a raquet-tailed drongo in flight, a black, fork-tailed bird whose little bunches of tail feathers were carried at the end of two thin plumes, looking as though the bird was being followed by a pair of winged beetles.

In the wet season when the jungle was humid from dense leafiness I'd be accompanied by the sound of frogs, invisible, but wheezing like congested lungs in different atonal keys. Sounds which once heard can be as instantaneous as smells in re-creating a particular place. I looked forward to riding in this season more than any other, in spite of the feeling of living in a sponge-bag left out in the sun. There was something so overwhelmingly verdant from the lush dripping tree canopy and the sense of muggy submersion into a green leafiness from layer beyond layer of reeking foliage.

Things should always be at extremes: who wants mediocrity – whether scrutinizing a bee on its honey quest or trying to encompass infinity? The fact that there are more stars in the universe than grains of sand on all the shores, sent me reeling the first time I read it. The furthest I can relate to time is when I'm in bed.

I sleep between linen sheets that were woven almost two hundred years ago. In fine cross-stitch, still clearly defined, is the date 1803, and embroidered under the date and the initials of the family is the number of the servant's bedroom to which each sheet belonged. (I assume the sheets were used by the servants, due to the lack of any embroidery or border along the upper edge.) The loom they were woven on must have been very narrow; down the centre of each sheet is a seam so finely oversewn the two halves lie flat. The weight of the linen, heavier than cotton, and the feel of these chalky-blue sheets which have survived so many generations, have an enduring reassurance as I fall asleep.

But sheets are ephemeral when compared to an olive tree. Contemplating an ancient tree which, like a yew, can live for fifteen hundred years or so, I am reminded of fossils not vegetation. The contorted trunk is as inert as rock; I put out my hand and touch deep fissures so primordial they have nothing to do with sappiness or the vitality of resurgence. Heirlooms of the Mediterranean, venerable and unyielding through endurance; my hand feels nothing but Homeric and encrusted antiquity.

Very aged wisterias have a similarly ossified appearance but it is the ginkgo, a tree with ornamental foliage turning golden in autumn and fruit which when crushed has a repulsive stench, that is the Methuselah of forest trees. A tree whose ancestry goes back through aeons, around one hundred and sixty million years, surviving unaltered through ice ages and vanishing reptiles.

This sense of the tree's intransigence is a mainstay in a world treated as expendable.

Making time stand still or slow up to a fraction of its usual speed is something Michael and I would deliberately set out to do. Regardless of the garden, we would travel not only to savour the pleasure of returning, but to play wizardry with time: we had the power to stop days running through our fingers like quicksilver. As soon as we left home we felt in control; we manipulated time to move at a snail's pace. Even a few days somewhere else, out of our usual context, and we felt we were living for weeks. Within twenty-four hours, yesterday seemed a long way behind us and time became elongated in a way which never happened at home, when weeks appeared as brief as days. Then, returning from some journey, Michael and I would anticipate with intense pleasure our first walk round the garden to see what particularly cherished plant was on the point of flowering. This anticipation never lost its edge.

There is no need to garden to appreciate gardens. Gardens have that dynamic. They work for people who wouldn't know a lupin from a marigold. And who cares? It isn't a matter of know-how, of recognizing plants or appreciating rareness, but of being, as Francis Bacon says, in a place to find the purest of human pleasures and a place to find refreshment to the spirit.

Now more than ever gardens are a lifeline for many who have never contemplated owning one themselves; they form a small calm eye in a world gone mad. When we are exposed daily to the horrors of the world through mass media coverage, until we become saturated to the point of desperation; when the vileness of mankind appears to be erupting in more countries than ever before and it is brought home to us relentlessly; when the decimation of the environment and wildlife is so catastrophic it affects not only the world but the individual, there comes a point when it's impossible to comprehend any more and for a moment's respite, it would be a relief if our imaginations atrophied.

We cannot take on the world, yet we cannot wish for impassivity or for the permanent loss of compassion which would allow us to sail through newspaper and TV reports with the same numbness as a visitor to India passes by the beggars. Are we at risk of becoming insensible? Whether we want to or not, have we each become a little

more thick-skinned since last year? Another disaster in India is common-place; it requires a deliberate pause in the business of getting up each morning to realize that the BBC reporter is referring to human beings before our self-protecting response comes up with: Oh, that again.

Fortunately mass communication also has placebos. Instantaneous involvement with something we're watching on TV can be restorative. I once watched an Australian documentary in which people gave up their time to refloat whales. Hundreds of volunteers, swarming like lemmings to the coast, submerged themselves in an icy sea in their effort to rescue sixty or so stranded creatures.

We watched how for days helpers of all ages stayed alongside the disorientated mammals, comforting and crooning, stroking and sooth-ing them. Time and again the creatures were washed back onto the shore, lying like giant blobs of tar the length of the beach, while the same people would patiently return to the animals' aid, by continually pouring water over them to prevent their skin from cracking, and by supporting their vast, displaced innards which pained the creatures as

they lay on land without the sea's buoyancy. In their attempts to head them out to sea the volunteers, guiding them like shepherds into deeper water, swam alongside the whales. Twice the great beasts, through some intuitive communication, turned back to the coast, to be once again stranded on the shore. Finally, on the third attempt, by hauling one whale as a decoy attached by rope to a boat, they succeeded in heading them away from the land into the deeper ocean, leaving behind their shepherds who were themselves by now lying on the beach spreadeagled and exhausted in sleep.

To every concave curve there's an equal convex one, so perhaps there's comfort from the fact that after the hurricane a few years back decaying forests offered regeneration to longhorn beetles, fungi and woodlice.

CHAPTER X

DAYS WITHOUT SHADOWS
Winter

W. H. Auden, the American poet, wrote 'In Memory of W. B. Yeats':

He disappeared in the dead of winter . . .
Far from his illness
The wolves ran on through the evergreen forests . . .

The words shudder, ringing with their own black testimony.

For a gardener can there be any words more cheerless than: 'Winter is over'? This is especially true if the winter has been unseasonal; when the mild weather has not only deprived us of a whole expanse of bleak impassivity, but has by its very moderation deceived the buds into opening, to be followed by carnage from a late frost. This deception is very unfunny – at times it can be heartbreaking. A magnolia and eucryphia, buddleja and *Hydrangea villosa* have all perished in the garden from cataclysmic cold.

Ronald Blythe, who writes so lucidly about his own garden, says that no gardener should dodge winter. Dodge winter? Who in their right mind wants to? A plummeting barometer and we wake to a silver garden. It is the only season for a gardener when the inner littorals of the mind can expand and non-colour leaves the enclosed eye mobile; when grey mould seeps through days of hynoptic tedium and we can stand aside and think distantly of the garden as if seeing it down the wrong end of a telescope. The blessing of monotony. We can view our gardens with the clarity of black and white photographs – their tonal distinctions as subtly varied as light on water, their identity refined to shape and structures. Stripped of flowers we can use a benedictory eye on bulk and mass, evergreens and water; twigs, bark, lichen, the grace of limbs and the patina of ageing.

A pelt of lightweight snow or a membrane of frost lying over the definitions of topiary are of more lasting imagery than any border in midsummer stridency. Winter is the unequivocal season; the one time in the year when we are not being got at by siren voices outside the window.

And more than any other season, winter is the time for reappraisal; for contemplation as we brood on the stark outlines and bony limbs of trees, when instinctively, without qualification or rational analysis, winter trees can bewitch the psyche. Resignation and bitter cold; the tones of nothingness, the stillness of December, are as pristine as an icicle; and by the turn of the year everything catastrophic can be eradicated, plant-lists remade, botches disguised, flowerbeds reshaped, until spring appears with its renewal of options.

Travel is a delightful con. Escaping, leaving everything behind and seeking fresh pastures appears conclusive. Yet already the first step out is the first step towards home. And now I find, without even needing to reach for my passport, that gardens have their own rhythmic cycle, inevitably returning me to where I started. The garden may be different each year – it is, of course – but the swing of the returning seasons is so reassuringly predictable it makes gardening an occupation of utter stability. Whatever disasters occur from month to month, working like Heffalump traps about the place into which I am bound to fall, I know that I shall be brought back to where I began by the turning year – and in particular to winter. Facing winter the fallen leaf is the first sign of spring.

Winter has charmed me ever since as a child I skated on one of the Norfolk Broads – those stretches of fresh water which once froze so hard but which seldom do now. The lakes were the result of ancient peat diggings where marsh harriers, bitterns and bearded tits inhabited the sedge. Now their lives are doomed: tourism and motor boats are menacing their existence and the birds live in peril of extinction in spite of what the conservationists are trying to do. But for us children the frozen waste became a miraculous dream where we skimmed like swallows over an icy sea – vast and boundless; the only sound was the swish of blades cutting the rough surface, the air was so cold it was painful to breathe, our bodies were warm and our fingers numb.

On the other side of the Broad were reed beds. Here, curving and tantalizing, were frozen lanes cut as passageways where the stems were annually harvested for thatch. And here we lost ourselves, drifting unseen in a silent emptiness overcome by icy annihilation. Those residual memories of childhood days are rooted so deep I can never be rid of winter. To assuage that longing to return, I used to spend hours looking at the scene within a glass ball which, when shaken, was transformed into a snowy phantasmagoria.

Years later I recaptured that miracle stillness when everything is pared to an icy simplicity. But this time it was snow: *ski de fond* in the Jura. The only sound above the noise of my own skis came when a competent skier overtook me with the swift hissing from his rhythmic speed. The trail led us over meadows, skirted farmsteads, sliced through dark forests and across snowswept uplands where the distant Alps, seen across Lac Léman, formed silhouettes so brittle they appeared to be barbed.

Snow and fog: for a gardener, surely, they are two of the most enigmatic winter weathers? Under snow the garden is transformed, blemishes vanish and everything recognizable – contours we have known, paths we used to walk, benches where we lingered – is turned into a cipher. But in fog an unearthly power dominates the garden among the looming trees and invisible boundaries. The ghostly outlines drift in and out of focus as we walk through our gardens, and vanish into thin air. In that anonymous landscape the garden is disguised; space and distance are alien as the freezing mist blots out everything familiar. Contemplation in winter is absolute; there are no fragmented anxieties from a demanding summer garden sizzling with colour.

I am confounded by the plants which share this desolation. Among them are hellebores. Even under snow, through which a few serrated

leaves have risen (opening later like a generous hand, palm upwards), the flowers keep breathing. They appear from such hopeless earth, these turbid hellebores reeking of the underworld with their murky petals, funereal and frail, the colours as quiet as bloom on damsons. The very sombreness of the flowers personifies winter.

Buttery-coloured winter aconites, rising hump-shouldered from the frigid ground and encircled by their green ruffs, inhabit churchyards with more constancy than they did my garden, with their tricky reluctance to become established. I was hoaxed by *Iris unguicularis* the first year I grew them. Where were the flowers I had been promised? Where was the violet-blue which was going to appear among a world of leaden greys? Reticent and secretive, their furled flowers were there, but concealed by a shield of spiky leaves.

Garrya elliptica, as long as you have the male plant of this large shrub or small tree, is constantly recommended as an invaluable evergreen for January, its catkins dangling with greeny-grey sobriety. But I was disappointed. One on its own did nothing for me, and I wish instead I had been bold and made a tunnel of garryas, so that in winter their oystery-coloured racemes would appear like delicate stalactites as I walked beneath. The rather lugubrious foliage could be threaded with clematis for later in the year.

A winter clematis I die for is *C. armandii*: evergreen and with leaves as tough as twill, it bears creamy flowers smelling faintly of vanilla and so spotless they defy commonsense when faced with glacial storms or the spatter of rain. Crocuses, of course, are lovely – but I grow them without much expectation of their surviving. One downpour reduces them to curdled pulp and yet their shape is so irresistible I succumb every year and plant another few handfuls.

The star among winter bulbs must surely be the snowdrop. There are certain gardeners for whom they are paramount, who admit to loving the flower above all others; smitten and resolute they will search for rare species in the dark days of the year, collecting all the varieties they can lay their hands on and hoarding them as acquisitively as others do sporting prints or Beatles memorabilia. And it's not hard to understand these obsessive galanthophiles; the flowers they are seeking have a furtive fragility which appeals to our quieter moods. The plant is small; yet it has an intangible magnetism from its unshowy, droop-headed flower with three oval petals overhanging the shorter petticoat arrangement within. Some snowdrops have about their whiteness the green luminosity of glaciers; some have a resoluteness to thrust through the earth, piercing dead leaves with their intent to flower. And others had us imagining we were hallucinating when, in November, in a small gully in northern Corfu under the shadow of olives, we found sprinklings of *Galanthus corcyrensis*. Their very names indicate how subjectively snowdrops have been seen in this country and abroad: Eve's Tears, Death's Flower, Fair Maids of February, *Nackte Jungfrau* and *Perce-neige*.

Heather Tanner wrote in her opening paragraph on snowdrops in *Woodland Plants*, which her husband Robin illustrated: 'Is there a creature so calloused that he has no special feeling for the snowdrop? Herein there is great hope for man, whatever his general depravity. The snowdrop has no colour, exhales a perfume so faint that it is usually detectable only by the early bees for which it is intended; it yields no salves or simples. It is loved partly for its bravery in thrusting through the winter soil, partly for its promise of the spring nowhere else apparent, but chiefly for its purity and innocence, and whoso is aware of that has in him poetry.' Pollinated by bees! It confounds logic. Yet if the snowdrops are late, the season mild, the bees early, pollination does take place, resulting in seed-pods dangling from the stems like miniature green eggs.

Gardeners have to believe that the dead will reincarnate. It is not only the plants that bloom with such perverse bravado that I love, but it's

also the dead black sticks of winter: those dismal affairs that inhabit the garden as witnesses of last year. Pick one. And know with absolute certainty at that moment you are holding summer. A hedgehog or tortoise keeps its recognizable form while hibernating; a rose reveals nothing. This hopeless-looking twig disguises its potential so that it is only by certainty in the cycle of seasons that we know that scent, shape and colour are contained within the unprepossessing object. Why, even in November, when the leaves of the *Hydrangea petiolaris* are scattering the ground, clearly visible are small buds as viridescent as pistachio nuts. Considering with confidence that things will become otherwise makes a wintry day in the garden wholly fulfilling.

I lament a snowless winter. I feel deprived as keenly as I would in a summer without roses. In the part of England where I live snow can no longer be taken for granted. But there were once days in the winter of 1950, when the brook was gagged with ice and the grey silhouettes of the alders stood gaunt along the stream, and Michael and I walked up onto the hill behind our village in search of snow. This was a time before the common grazing land had been fenced to prevent stock from wandering along the lanes. There was no need; few people had cars, only an occasional bus or lumbering tractor, the kind that looked like Disneyland crustaceans, passed by.

On our way up to the hill we passed sheep straggling down in their search for food. Above the snow line, where the hill ponies bunched together, their coats rough and encrusted as rind is on a mature cheese, we walked over ground as hard as nails. With aching ears and our breath fuming into dissolving plumes, we looked down onto the countryside towards the distant rise and fall of Wenlock Edge and beyond to Wales, where the sulky light smudged outlines, emphasizing the farouche quality of winter.

On other days, when snowdrifts on the hill were treacherous, rising like waves frozen on the point of breaking, I used to ride my horse along the lanes, cantering silently through snow too deep for wheels – long before snowploughs, followed by the gritter, were used to keep the roads open. In wintry desolation, between hedges drooping from the weight of snow, I'd occasionally have to stop to clear the snow balling up on the mare's hooves. The quality of non-entity on those rides was total. Only the warmth of my horse, her smell and her chestnut neck and the faint creak of the saddle were signs that anything moved or lived in that white void. Since then I've seldom felt that sense of vacant suspension when time, pressure, otherness or momentum were absent; when there is a feeling of being both the perceiver and the perceived. The mood is way beyond the limitation of words. Known only to myself, the thought is dead before it's formed. Only now and then, during a lull in the garden, have I felt that momentary sense of passive release as I did on those singular rides in winter.

I wonder what it is about winter which so mesmerizes some of us? I am not alone. There are others who feel as I do. Take Robert Frost.

Presumably it was not just his name that aroused him to write so many poems about winter. Then there's Keats. Keats's opening lines of 'The Eve of St Agnes' are piercingly evocative:

St Agnes' Eve – Ah, bitter chill it was!
The owl, for all his feathers, was a-cold;
The hare limp'd trembling through the frozen grass,
And silent was the flock in woolly fold.

Among the literary giants here is Proust in this majestic flow of prose in one continuous sentence, so dense, so fervent, and because it is pivoting on something as ephemeral as violets in winter Proust has us subjected. We cannot but be moved by such eloquence:

Could I even have made them understand the emotion that I used to feel on winter mornings, when I met Madame Swann on foot, in an otter-skin coat, with a woollen cap from which stuck out two blade-like partridge-feathers, but enveloped also in the artificial warmth of her own house, which was suggested by nothing more than the bunch of violets crushed into her bosom, whose flowering, vivid and blue against the grey sky, the freezing air, the naked boughs, had the same charming effect of using the season and the weather merely as a setting, and of living actually in a human atmosphere, in the atmosphere of this woman, as had in the vases and jardinières of her drawing-room, beside the blazing fire, in front of the silk-covered sofa, the flowers that looked out through closed windows at the falling snow?

Brueghel set his peasants and hunters with their lean and brutish figures against a Flemish wintry landscape; the American artist Andrew Wyeth used a spare style when painting his naturalistic winter scenes and Pissaro caught the reflected light in his scene of winter in Upper Norwood. But it is Alfred Sisley's shadowless masterpiece, 'Snow at Louveciennes', which captivates for me an urban winter. The year is

1874, and a quality of silence and the anaemia of winter surrounds the figure of a woman as she walks towards us shielding herself with an umbrella from a few snowflakes idling through the air.

Edward Lear also caught a winter light in his watercolours of Corfu. On an evening when the day had been clear, when the mainland appeared closer – almost within touching distance from the purity of the air – when the sea, motionless all day, looked more like silk than water, then as the sun went down there was a moment when the straits between the island and mainland turned to 'lavender water tinged with pink'. Edward Lear transferred to paper that extraordinary pellucidity, that quality at sunset which, even as we looked, melted into mauve and cobalt dissolving into darkness.

The transforming force in gardens is undeniable. Not what we do to a garden, but what it does to us. Self-discovery, tranquillity, meditation or fulfilment – any one of these effects can overcome a gardener intent on planting euphorbia or inhaling sweet balsam. A painter, one with a truly botanical knowledge as to how a flower grows, also finds this transforming force as he or she puts down on paper the sense of vitality intrinsic to a flower, whether they use a naturalistic form or represent the abstract quiddity of a plant.

'The force that through the green fuse drives the flower' is powerfully captured by certain painters, making the veracity of their paintings almost visionary, almost resonant. Surely, only a painter who has looked at and assimilated the essence of the flower, could paint like that? Using photographs, copying from books or from other artists' work, can never have the same result as where the artist, painting from life, has been kindled by the primal green fuse which Dylan Thomas writes about.

Elizabeth Blackadder's clear brushwork in her watercolour of 'Fallen Tulips', so beautifully catching the ephemeral quality of flowers a breath away from decay, has more embodiment of the spirit of the bulbs than the tulips shedding their petals in my courtyard.

The Australian artist Margaret Stones may be an exemplary draughtsman with her illustrations for the *Botanical Magazine*, but her own perception of a particular flower, the quality she finds there, shows almost a sense of homage towards her model. And the same fidelity appeared centuries earlier in a Japanese painting of a tree peony on silk, or a Chinese painting of a lotus rising flawless from some muddy depth. (When we lived in Thailand we marvelled to see how unsullied the lotus buds emerged from the filthy squalor of some of the *klongs* of Bangkok – canals which have long since been filled in.)

The highly technical accomplishment of photographic flower portraits, which seems to have proliferated at the speed of light the last few years, is brilliant and wonderful. The effect of homing-in with the camera on a single flower has a totally different impact from that of recording a group of rose, clematis and verbascum, where the camera's discriminatory eye eliminates some dreadful flower combination further down the bed, or from a wide-angled view of a garden where we can savour, or not, the gardener's sense of design. Look at Andrew Lawson's close-up photograph of a single flower on a *Magnolia grandiflora*, where the stamens, like finely carved ivory, are held within the cupped fragility and the brittle rims of petals surrounded by glossy, black-green leaves. The photograph has the consummate perfection of light, sensuality and definition (which an artist also portrays), without having that final dimension which a painting can reveal but which a photograph, however sensitive, cannot. Look at a portrait, for instance, of Joseph Raffael's. Here the American artist has painted the frilly lips of an orchid with almost erotic reverence, and reveals a threatening power from the oversized flowers which appear to be reflexing their petals even as you look.

Portraits of flowers can sustain a gardener through the winter with more propulsion than any nurseryman's catalogue, however esoteric or

pictorial the production. Flower paintings work like an anthology: like verse to flit and skim through, picking up good vibes from this one or that one, dismissing others, and from some, from the really inspired artists, finding in their work something so intangible, yet so authentic, they reflect the arcane mysticism of gardens.

It is October now as I am finishing this book. I know what lies ahead: in two weeks our clocks will go back, the days will shorten, until by four in the afternoon the curtains are closed and the garden obliterated from sight. Those who live for their gardens will be downcast, shattered to contemplate months of inactivity when often the ground is either too squelchy or too frozen to attempt a half-day's tidying-up; when rain, fog or gloom prevent even a little devotional ship-shapeness about the place. But seen differently these four months are a godsend; a reprieve, a time for reformation, a time when the garden lies like the calm eye in a storm. You know it's there but it remains serenely quiescent; ahead is the one season when you will belong to yourself.

Love of gardens in winter has nothing to do with sagacity, of intellect or rationality. The feeling is far deeper than reason. Perhaps the mystery of winter is emptiness. The quality of pause. The lack of striving and the sense of receptivity. Walk into your garden and you will find that all the havoc of summer is so distant it is almost impossible to recapture even the memory of a pulse. And I think it is then, at the nadir of the year, that a great sense of cessation is so profound I feel no impatience for December to move into January.

Illustrations

Many of the illustrations are taken from the author's collection of old gardening books, and from some kindly lent by David Wheeler. Others are reproduced by kind permission of the artists: Simon Dorrell, *127*; Gertrude Hermes (especial thanks to Judith Russell), *54, 63, 110, 128, 143, 145, 150, 154, 159*; Pamela Hughes, *51*; Miriam Macgregor, *17, 74, 86, 91, 96, 105*; Brian Partridge, *31*; Howard Phipps, *21, 49, 112, 172*; Monica Poole, *41, 60, 165*; Yvonne Skargon, *53, 101, 152, 162, 166, 169, 174*; Edward Stamp, *77*; Lesley Sutherland, *161*; Christopher Wormell, *135*.